The Overachiever's Guide to

GETTING
UNSTUCK

Replan, Reprioritize, Reaffirm

William L. Reeb, CPA/CITP, CGMA

Notice to Readers

The Overachiever's Guide to Getting Unstuck: Replan, Reprioritize, Reaffirm does not represent an official position of the American Institute of Certified Public Accountants, and it is distributed with the understanding that the author and publisher are not rendering legal, accounting, or other professional services in the publication. If legal advice or other expert assistance is required, the services of a competent professional should be sought.

For information about the procedure for requesting permission to make copies of any part of this work, please email copyright@aicpa.org with your request. Otherwise, requests should be written and mailed to the Permissions Department, AICPA, 220 Leigh Farm Road, Durham, NC 27707-8110.

1 2 3 4 5 6 7 8 9 0 PIP 1 9 8 7 6 5 4 3

ISBN: 978-1-93735-287-5

Publisher: Linda Prentice Cohen
Acquisition Editor: Erin Valentine
Developmental Editor: Andrew Grow

CONTENTS

Preface

The First Question

The first question everyone asks me when I mention this book is, "What is it about?" Simply put ... this book was written to help you get more out of your life. For some of the overachievers I have worked with over the past 30 years, "more" to them could best be summed up as getting better, faster, and stronger. For others, it has been about creating greater life balance: balance between numerous time intensive functions like work, family, health, happiness, and spiritual activities. And finally for some, it has been about creating clarity and priority regarding the many ideas and expectations that constantly bombard them so that they are better equipped to focus their time and energy on what is truly important to them. So, from here forward, as shorthand, I commonly frame all three of these variations of progress ("more," "balance," and "clear priorities") as achieving greater success and happiness. I believe the key to accomplishing this is learning how to maintain your momentum, and when you start losing it or get stuck, learning how to quickly get unstuck, making progress again toward whatever it is you are trying to achieve.

Why Overachiever?

I decided to focus on the overachiever for a number of reasons. The first is because I am an overachiever myself, struggling with the various points raised in this text, so I can relate well to this group. The second is because this is a term that best classifies the vast majority of the clients that I counsel. They are so driven, and they so casually set lofty goals for themselves that they get trapped by their own plans, expectations, and priorities. Based on my work with overachievers, they often have trouble

- creating balance in their lives.

- not defaulting to being a martyr who commonly tries to satisfy too many conflicting demands rather than prioritizing and expending energy on what is really important to them and learning to let go of the other lesser important demands.

- determining when enough is enough. This comes in two forms. The first is that this group commonly sets new objectives for themselves about the time they start to see the possibility of reaching the existing ones, often putting excessive and constant pressure on themselves to perform. The second is that they can almost become obsessive compulsive about achieving perfection regarding one goal at the sacrifice of other equally important goals.

Another reason I chose this term is because the word "overachiever" embodies both a positive and negative connotation. For example, the definition of "overachiever" in The American Heritage® Dictionary of the English Language, Fifth Edition:

Overachievers are individuals who "perform better or achieve more success than expected" ... "Achieve more success than expected" is the positive view.

On the negative side, there is a presumption that the "overachiever" is achieving those results through an excessive, unreasonable or unwarranted effort.

So the perception here is that the overachiever, while achieving superior results, expends a great deal of marginally productive, or wasted, energy and effort compared to the gain realized. Overachievers, because of their high-achievement mentality, are positioned to get stuck more often than others because of their constant evaluation of their progress as compared to expectation as well as their frustration with anything other than performance excellence. The problem is that anytime anyone is trying to develop new skills, capabilities or understanding in uncharted territory, that person's expected progress or preconceived excellence in performance is often misguided and unrealistic. Therefore, this group is the perfect audience for the techniques and concepts outlined in this book either to keep them from getting stuck in the first place, or to help them get unstuck.

Everyone Needs a Sage

Before we dive into the material, I want to highlight a few people that have been instrumental in the evolution of this book. Everyone needs a *sage*. I am very lucky because I have two. A sage to me is that person who is wise beyond his or her years, is there to help you, who can see the real you, who can help *you* see the real you, and has a desire for you to be happy and successful in your life. My wife, Michaelle, who you will hear about throughout this book, is one of my sages. Her primary desire is for me to be happy. And as you will find out from my stories, she has a way of cutting through the fog to help me see areas I need to address or change.

Michaelle and I, at least for the last 15 years, have had a deep commitment to each other to support any activities that promote a healthier body, both physically and mentally. For Michaelle, that turns out to be walking or hiking (depending on the venue) and yoga, with both activities occurring on most days. For me, that healthy activity is mainly martial arts. I originally decided to get involved in martial arts because I was seeking an aerobic activity that I could be involved in for decades that would simultaneously be developing a valuable set of skills (self-defense skills). It was the perfect overachiever alternative—one effort accomplishing two important tasks. Today, while staying in shape is an important part of my being able to maintain a balanced life, martial arts has evolved beyond just being a skill and has become more about the way I think and process my choices.

Given the importance of martial arts in my life, as you could expect, my adventure led me to another sage. His name is John Blankenship and he has evolved from being my instructor to being a good friend, but most important, a mentor. John and I, through entirely separate careers, life choices and experiences, discovered that we were both teaching our audiences the same basic concepts. My path was through business by helping owners create and implement strategy, leverage opportunities or resolve problems. John's path was through martial arts, helping individuals learn self-mastery, self-control, and health of the mind and body. At first it appeared that our professions had little in common (martial arts training versus management consulting), and the terminology we were using to express various concepts also didn't seem to connect. As my development evolved, and as I grew to better understand what John was teaching, I was able to see how the concepts taught at his school were similar to those I was teaching in business. The major theme to this discovery, which I will abbreviate with the phrase "it's all the same," is commonly shortened in martial arts venues even further to "same-same" (a theme I leverage throughout the book). I had heard this phrase over and over from three different martial arts masters over a 30-year period. However, with John's regular coaching, one day I finally got it and I was able to understand what they had all been trying to tell me. What I found common among martial arts, my business and personal life experiences, my athletic endeavors, and my relationships was this:

> *Regardless of what I was doing, similar techniques and concepts could be applied to each situation that would improve the likelihood of my achieving the results or desired outcomes I was seeking.*

As an example of same-same, consider one of John's school mantras "feet, center, and martial intent" (a concept more fully explained later in the book). Whether I am executing a kick in Tae Kwon Do, a joint lock in Hapkido, or a talon rake in Hun Gar, I still have to keep my mind focused on my three points of attention (I need to feel my feet connected to the ground, balance myself over my center and strike with martial intent). Whether I am about to hit an approach shot to a green in golf or ski down steep terrain in the snow, my success thoughts regarding execution needed to be the same; stay aware of how my feet are connected to the ground (feet), maintain my balance (center), and don't be passive in my efforts (martial intent). And whether I am about to give a speech to 1,000 conference attendees or facilitate an intimate personal development session with a small group of leaders, I have to remain grounded by my core values (feet), manage my insecurities and ego to balance my emotions (center), and work with intense passion regarding whatever I am doing (martial intent).

Once the same-same was clear, the idea of creating this book was formed. After many discussions with John, this book now conceptualizes a combination of "critical techniques to engage" and "concepts to consider" that can more consistently help you find the success and happiness you are looking for. Over the past few years, I have paid special attention to those techniques and concepts I call upon when counseling others that have had the greatest impact. From this research and our discussions, John and I put together the Process outlined in this book. It will help ou cut through your own personal chaos and clutter to open a clearer path for you to achieve the "more" you are looking for. And just as important, I believe that this book can offer insight into how you can find greater joy during your day-to-day self-improvement process. In order to demonstrate how the various techniques and concepts covered apply to whatever you are focusing on, I have purposely rotated my examples using personal life experiences, sports, martial arts, and business situations to show "it is all the same."

A Note of Perspective

Many people have played a part in the development of this book, from John's coaching and concepts, to Michaelle who has read and critiqued this book start to finish almost as many times as I have (not to mention the role she has played in my life), to my partner Dom Cingoranelli providing his perspective of more than 30 years of training people in leadership and management, to Sean Cavins, the martial arts master that mentors me during my frequent stays in Colorado, and the many others including Carter Heim, Mark Hildebrand, Eric Rigby, Janet Overton, Karen Price, Matt Andersen, Arleen Thomas, Allyson Baumeister, Deborah Curry, Susan Roberts who have read this manuscript through its many evolutions and provided me with detailed commentary as to how to improve it. However, without John's advice, guidance and support throughout the development process of this manuscript, this book would not exist. For that motivation, John deservedly is listed as the "Concept Visionary and Sage" for this book.

Finally, I want to thank the AICPA and its professional team for taking on this project. While there are too many people to acknowledge, my first thoughts are of Amy Plent who believed in this project enough to get us to contract. And I can't leave out Andrew Grow and Erin Valentine who delivered essential guidance, exceptional patience, and unparalled professionalism throughout this project.

Given this short preamble—without further ado—it is time to allow the Process to unfold.

Introduction

A Quick View of the Process

It's time to take a quick overview of the Process that fills the remaining chapters of this book.

I was looking for a process that was logical, yet would be dynamic enough to respond to life as it unfolds around us. For example, when I am hired to help an organization create a strategy and then implement it, I call upon a formal process to get us from vision through execution. However, often the reason I am called in the first place is because someone or some organization realizes they are stuck. When this is the case, I first take a look at where they are, what they have already done or attempted, where they want to go, and then help them see for themselves what next action will likely unstick them so they can continue moving again in the direction of their choice. The steps in this system follow a logical flow and are shared in a flow chart built as we go through the book.

In the following paragraphs, I will introduce the techniques and concepts within the Process that are designed to help you find whatever success or happiness you are looking for. The following paragraphs outline all of this from a 30,000 foot level as the concepts are more fully developed within the chapters that follow.

The first step is to identify what it is that you desire. Desire is at the core of the process. Being stuck, or for that matter getting unstuck, will require you to cycle back to it. Zig Ziglar once said, "If you aim at nothing, you will hit it every time." So, this question is straight-forward ... "What are you aiming at?" While this question might seem simple, what we believe we are willing to do to achieve our desire is often far from what we are actually willing to do. So, we have to sift through a lot of chaos and clutter to find that truth. Chapter 2, "Desire," has two sections; the first is "Techniques to Consider as You Begin to Identify Your Desires" and the second is "Considerations as You Create Your Plan." After reviewing the first section and giving some thought to what you want, the next section helps you think about your plan, tactics for that plan (with a realistic timeline), and reasonable expectations. By putting together this level of detail, you will be able to better frame the effort you are about to make and compare that against the gains you expect to receive. If you find yourself unwilling to put together your plan, your identified desire is likely just a "wish" and the process stalls out until you either (1) actually become ready to put your plan and tactics together, or (2) redefine your desire into something that is in line with the effort you are willing to make. There is nothing wrong with wishes, but this book is about helping overachievers focus their talent and energy so they can get more of what they really want.

Once you have a plan outlined to accomplish what you want, then the next step is to start doing the Work. The work is about putting in the required consistent sustained self-motivated effort to achieve whatever you are trying to accomplish. I have broken this topic into two sections; one focused on techniques to sustain the work and the other on how to work better, faster, and smarter. Many people have an idyllic or a romanticized view of what it takes to get better, faster, and stronger, or get "more," and they won't mentally or physically "chop the wood" necessary to get it done. When you reach an evaluation point and find you are no longer willing to do the required work, or you become dis-satisfied with your progress or priorities, or you determine that the gains you are achieving no longer justify the effort, you will either be stuck or will be starting to get stuck. At this juncture, when you realize that you are either feeling unsuccessful or unhappy about the progress or direction you are heading, it is time for you to reassess "What You *Are* Thinking" and "What You *Are* Doing" to position yourself to make the necessary adjustments so that you can get back on course and regain your momentum.

In many simple cases or situations, the overachiever is fully committed, ready and capable of staying focused until the success or happiness sought after is achieved. If that is where you are, identifying a desire (which includes planning, plan tactics and expectations) and doing the work, is all there is to the Process. But as all overachievers know, we get distracted by the many conflicting demands and unrealistic expecta-tions we put on ourselves, so simple situations can become complex very quickly. Therefore, when we take on too much, or we find ourselves running like hamsters on a wheel to nowhere, it is time to determine which actions are necessary to effect any change in the way we think or what we do.

John and I have identified three actions that can help you get unstuck. They are

> **Replan**: We can change the desire (which might mean changing some aspect of the plan or its tactics, timeline, and expectations) to align with what we now know that we want

> **Reprioritize**: We can reprioritize what is important to us in order to remove any conflict in ideas, values, beliefs that are getting in the way of our making progress

> **Reaffirm**: We can disconnect the emotional link between our desire and progress so that even when a negative evaluation occurs, our feelings don't get in our way of working towards our goals

Each of these actions can be taken to resolve the dissatisfaction you are experiencing and allow you to start moving again. By identifying your desires and doing the work, and, when necessary, replanning, reprioritizing, or reaffirming, you will find this process to be a very powerful tool to help you achieve. It provides you with an arsenal of techniques at your disposal to propel you forward towards your objective, whether that is achieving a goal, progressing in your ability or understanding, enjoying greater satisfaction, finding a new level of happiness, or getting "more" out of your life. The summary graphic shown here represents an overview of the Process, which will be broken down and displayed in greater detail as we work through the chapters below.

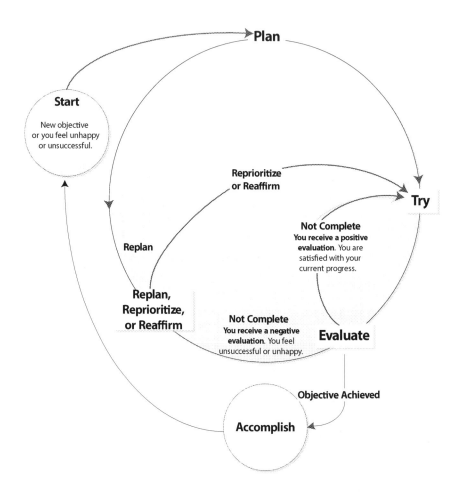

The Roadblocks We Encounter

It's funny ... every business I have counseled is different, yet fundamentally they are all dealing with some of the same basic issues. And while every individual I work with is unique, I also find that we are all fundamentally similar (just another reflection of the concept "same-same").

It is common for overachievers to wrestle with accomplishment expectations that cause us to reevaluate who we are, who we aspire to be, whether our existence has made a difference to anyone, if we will ever live up to our idealized self-image, and more. What makes this self-analysis or self-report even more difficult is that each of us also has to try to separate our own true feelings and beliefs from those emotions and values we unquestionably adopt from influential groups that are part of our lives, such as

1. family, teachers, mentors, employers, or others one aspires to emulate.

2. someone you want to "gain" something from, whether that be love, affirmation, advancement, money, gift, approval, and so on

3. personally developed standards like ethical/moral constructs, service/devotional beliefs and more.

The point is ... we are complex. As is often said, we are like onions with layers and layers of protective skin, making it difficult to find the core. With each layer we peel back, though on one hand we might be closer to uncovering the truth of who we are, we might also just be uncovering another layer of disorienting chaos and clutter. For example, I am a CPA by profession. Did I choose that profession because it was who I saw myself to be early on in my life? Was it because of someone I knew that I wanted to emulate? Perhaps I am a CPA because this career synced with a personal ethic or belief. Maybe I thought my parents would be proud of me. It is often very hard to identify the difference between what we really want versus what we believe we want in order to satisfy (1) those we care about, (2) those we aspire to please or prove wrong, or (3) beliefs and values we have embraced. Our quest for understanding is made even more difficult because the people who influence us, as well as our beliefs, change as we evolve throughout life. For example, have you ever met someone who had faith and then lost it, or someone who found faith? In both of these cases, those people's belief systems were torn apart and rebuilt on opposite extremes. As you can imagine, for all of us, determining what we want out of life is not as straight-forward as it would seem.

As you might guess from the little I have covered so far, I believe that one of our biggest roadblocks is our unwillingness to peel back our protective layers until we can determine what drives or hinders us. Are you willing to unpeel enough layers so that you can finally separate what actions and beliefs you embrace merely to gratify others versus those you welcome to satisfy your own needs and desires? To find a sustainable bridge to our own success and happiness, each of us should take the time to identify what is truly important us rather than just default to societal norms and pressures. For instance, young couples are often pressured by family and friends to start having children immediately after they marry. It is not uncommon for friends, family, community, and support groups, without negative intent and with love in their hearts, to create an extra load for the couple to carry by laying down guilt, duty, fear, and other emotional baggage in order to convince them to have children immediately. This couple may have other aspirations at this stage of their lives, like climbing a career ladder, traveling the world, or just enjoying the freedom of being unencumbered youth in love. But in the face of confusion, lack of clarity of direction or priorities, or pressure, this young couple often will embark on the path desired for them by others. I have heard over the years from a number young professionals that they believed had they had chosen a path of their own, they would have been perceived as "selfishly indulging" themselves rather than growing up. Just so you know, this example is not about when or whether anyone should have children—that is each person's individual choice. But what this example is trying to point out is ... others truly don't know what is best for you or what will give you the greatest satisfaction. The decision to have children early may work out perfectly, but it also might also expedite an early divorce if the couple allowed others to overly influence the direction and priorities of their lives.

Overachievers, because we are regularly trying to surpass the expectations of those around us, are overly susceptible to the influence of others. Often we take on a mindset of martyrdom with the internal thought, "Well, I can just work a little harder and longer so that my efforts will create a result that will satisfy them too." The lesson here is: Stop Thinking Like That! Don't routinely sacrifice the limited time in your life to making everyone else happy while deferring your own success and happiness until such a time in the future when everyone else has been taken care of.

Please understand this: The best person to determine what is important to you is *you*! Others, if they have taken the time to do their own self-analysis, should know what is best for them. However, that awareness in no way makes them experts on how you should focus your efforts or spend your life. Only you can determine what you really want. And if you are not confident, then the answer is not to chastise yourself for not knowing, nor is it to simply follow the direction of the support group around you, but rather for you to start taking steps every day to peel back enough layers of your own onion to see and feel your own truth. This book should provide a great deal of insight as to how to maneuver around, over, and through the many roadblocks you can expect to find along your path, including what you need to do the next time you find yourself stuck or starting to get stuck.

Let Go of What You Think You Know

"Let go of what you think you know" is something John's students say and read every time we enter the school to train; it is a fundamental idea to embrace if you want to expand your ability to learn and grow. This phrase is a reminder to ensure that your existing knowledge and skill do not negatively impact your willingness to gain new knowledge and skill!

It's funny how we think, sometimes. For example, it is not uncommon that we position ourselves on either end of a spectrum (I know something or I don't; I have a skill or I don't). When people think they already know something, it is hard to even get their attention to consider new ideas unless they believe someone else knows more than they do. The same is true for a skill. When people are highly skilled, in many situations, until you can prove that you can perform at a higher level than they can, they will often close their mind to any new information you are sharing (it's like you don't have the right to give constructive feedback or provide a different perspective unless you are better skilled or more knowledgeable than the person you are speaking to).

In John's school, as part of the school oath, students used to say, "Respect your seniors." This actually fell in line with the common notion mentioned previously that we should show respect to the people who have risen to a level of competency above ours. However, about 10 years ago, that phrase was changed simply to "Respect Others." As part of our learning pedagogy and as a black belt, I am commonly critiqued by lower belts, including white belts that might only have a few weeks of experience. At first, this shift in thinking was humbling. Why, after 20 years of training, would I respectfully receive corrections or sug-gested improvements from someone with only months of experience? The answer is—someone doesn't have to be more capable than you to help you get better! I can tell you from years of practice, though that inexperienced white belt may not have the background to perform the complex movement I might be demonstrating, he or she can almost always provide insight as to some gross movement they saw that looked inconsistent, unfocused, or unbalanced. Their almost naive perspective often contains some incredibly valuable insight.

Just thinking about this reminds me of an old story, maybe even an urban myth, that General Electric would ask each of its newly hired engineers to solve the problem of smoothing the bright spot out of the light bulb. The existing engineers, knowing that this problem could not be solved, thought this was an excellent hazing exercise and a humbling experience to remind these new recruits just how little they actually knew. However, as you know today, there is no singular bright spot in a light bulb. Someone solved the problem, proving to the experienced engineers that people taking a fresh look at a problem, even with limited experience, have a wonderful perspective to share. Whether or not this example is actually true is irrelevant. I can tell you that in a business setting, I will often charge people in new roles, or people that are new in their jobs, to look at processes or approaches and share their improvement opinions. Because these people were not party to creating the existing processes or approaches, they have no vested interest (and therefore no filter) in trying to find a way to support the current solutions. Because they are looking at the situation without a lot of preconceived notions as to what has, should, or will work, these people are predisposed to letting go of what they think they know and taking a fresh objective look with open eyes and an open mind.

The lesson here is ... as soon as you think you know something, you might subconsciously be putting up barriers to your learning. Therefore, if you want to get better, faster, and stronger, a first step I am suggesting is to let go of what you think you know.

A different view of this same idea is realize that you are limited in what you *can* know because of your current level of knowledge and experience. For instance, I used to think that when I became a black belt, I would know almost everything about a particular martial art and that all of my focus could then shift toward fine tuning those various techniques. What I can tell you now, with certainty, is that I saw a far brighter knowledge and skill light at the end of the tunnel in my first few years of training than I can see right now, more than 20 years later. I have only scratched the surface of what there is to learn and my skills are almost infantile in the evolution of what they could be. In other words, with each opportunity to learn or grow we position ourselves to be able to see the more that is there. To me, it is almost the height of arrogance to state that we *know* anything without adding this annotation:

> "Anytime I state that I know something, the statement is made based on my current level of skill, knowledge, experience, biases, personal baggage, attitudes and prejudices. As my knowledge and experience are enhanced, I could easily find out that what I thought I knew, I didn't even know at all because at that time I was not far enough along in my development to fully comprehend the limitations of my awareness or perceptions."

Several months ago, we were going over one of the Korean forms, which I learned seven or eight years ago, from the Tae Kwon Do discipline. I have observed, commented on, and taught this form for years to other students in the interim. However, that day, John broke down the form in a different way to re-teach a group of instructors. John maintained that this update was to simply focus on a few spots in the form that needed additional insight. As someone relearning the form that day, I would say that there were but a few movements that remained unchanged. So, here was a form that I thought I already knew and had taught to others now being re-taught to me. However, this time around I was provided a more detailed perspective of the techniques, their intent, and what the opponent might be doing to counter each movement. So, realizing that you are limited in what you *can* know because of your current level of knowledge and experience predisposes you to let go of what you think you know.

These were hard philosophies for me to embrace because as an overachiever I have always been proud of what I have been able to accomplish as well as the depth and breadth of my experience. In a way, these philosophies diminish all of that. However, adopting them has allowed me to more easily let down my guard and defensiveness so that I am positioned to see things from an entirely new perspective. So, don't settle into a viewpoint that encourages you to think you have finally acquired all the requisite knowledge or skill that you need regarding any aspect of your life. That kind of finality is created for comfort and vanity. Instead, realize that knowledge, skills, values, beliefs and experiences are simply part of your constantly evolving awareness. Keep learning ... Keep growing ... Keep doing the work!

This book and the materials in it have become integrated into the way I think. Each day, I need to be ready to let go of what I think I know so that I am better mentally prepared to learn more. Don't read this book as if the concepts discussed here represent some kind of final truth, because you will not find that here. The narrative is simply my perspective right now, which I hope continually evolves. But just because what I understand today will continue to change, that doesn't mean that what I have to share isn't valuable. Based on the results of John's and my helping thousands of people positively reshape their lives, I am asking you to let go of what you think you know long enough to take in the ideas, techniques, and concepts covered in the following chapters because they absolutely can help you find greater happiness, peace of mind, success or the "more" you are looking for in your life. To clarify the importance of this idea, I believe you will be wasting your time reading any further or attempting to apply the techniques described if you are not sincerely willing to let go of what you think you know. By processing the contents of this book without this willingness, I believe that rather than experiencing any profound changes in the way you think or in what you do, you will simply be adding more information and perpetuating the same obstacles and situations you are experiencing now.

A Note on Organization

I organized this book in a manner similar to how I have been taught martial arts. First, you are introduced to techniques and then asked to practice (in this case, give thought to) those techniques. Once you become familiar with them, the next step is to allow those techniques to logically lead into a broader application of concepts that you can personalize and incorporate into your everyday thinking. Eventually, through practice and utilization, they will become part of your instinctive reaction to your everyday experiences.

I also provided an organizational aid to help you determine which techniques might be most valuable to you at the time of this reading. Recognize that each time you read this book, assuming you call upon this text again, based on what you are trying to achieve in your life, your assessment as to what is relevant to you will likely change. This is because where you are getting stuck or are stuck will change, so what might help you get unstuck today versus unstuck tomorrow will likely change as well. Therefore, after the discussion of each technique, I have inserted two short exercises for you to work through. I first ask you to assess how you are performing in the area just covered. In other words, rate whether you believe you have been or are experiencing some aspect of "stuckness" regarding the idea just discussed. If you are, then you are getting a clue as to something you might need to let go of. Then, I ask you to follow up that rating with how you might apply that particular technique to help you start making progress again regarding whatever objective you have in mind.

I don't expect each idea to apply or be valuable to you at any particular reading. Remember, the various techniques and concepts are designed so that as you work through them, you should find yourself thinking differently about whatever it is you are struggling with. For those ideas that seem applicable, I am asking that you let down your guard, let go of what you think you know, and consider how you might be able to put one or a combination of them to work for you immediately. And for those ideas that seem unsuitable, as I just mentioned, ignore them for now, but don't totally dismiss them as they might be exactly what you need at some point in the near future. At least that has been my personal experience!

Chapter 1
Getting Stuck or Being Stuck

What Does "Getting Stuck" or "Being Stuck" Mean?

Based on experiences in my own life and decades working as a coach and consultant to very successful business executives and owners, getting more out of your life often comes down to how quickly you recognize and respond to the early warning signs like losing momentum, suffering from diminishing returns on your efforts, or experiencing the disconnect between what you are thinking and what you want to do. Overachievers get stuck regularly. For us, this is simply life in action. The question isn't whether this will happen to you, but rather, "Is it happening to you right now?" And if the answer is "Yes," that is not a big deal. But what can easily become a big deal is remaining stuck. My experience with overachievers is that we have a problem being idle, so we are going to expend our energy doing something. The problem is that "something" we do often resembles our being hamsters on a wheel—running hard to nowhere—rather than using our energy to achieve what is really important to us. So when you get stuck, which you will, this book should help you see early-on the techniques or concepts you can apply to get yourself off the hamster wheel and back on course to your objectives. At the center of this positive transformation will be your willingness to let go of what you think you know, which might be a priority or weight of a belief or value as compared to another or an unrealistic expectation or something. The more diligently and relentlessly you hold on to everything you are currently thinking and doing, the more likely you are to get stuck and stay stuck because you are not looking for answers, *you are merely looking for validation.*

Early Warning Signals of Getting Stuck

As my martial arts Master, John, and I discussed the idea of getting or being stuck, we identified several common early warning signals that are often a precursor to feeling unsuccessful in what you are trying to achieve or unhappy about your progress or priorities. These were the most common:

- **Losing Momentum** (Slowing Progress: when doing the Work, committing the effort, and achieving Progress are no longer in congruence with each other). Just the idea (the way you think) that you might be losing momentum is often enough to trigger dissatisfaction.

- **Diminishing Returns** (Negligible Progress: when an indirect relationship starts to exist between doing the Work and achieving Progress, or said another way, the Work disproportionately increases in relationship to Progress achieved). Extended effort against diminishing gain is enough to trigger dissatisfaction.

- **Functional Disconnect** (No Progress: when Desire is in direct conflict with your priorities (an idea, belief, value) making it difficult or impossible to do the Work until the disconnect is resolved). Your inability to move because of the conflict between what you are thinking and what you want or plan to do will create huge dissatisfaction.

Each of these is remedied through replanning, reprioritizing or reaffirming, but if not addressed, will eventually lead to the same result: getting stuck or being stuck. As you might surmise, there is a severity difference between the early warning signals with each leading to dissatisfaction.

The highest level of severity occurs when you are experiencing a functional disconnect because you most likely will be very dissatisfied and stuck. If you are suffering from diminishing returns, while less severe because you are still likely to be making small incremental progress, the time and resources required to sustain additional progress is probably way out of balance. This imbalance typically is the source of a great deal of frustration and, unaddressed, will eventually lead to being stuck. Losing momentum, though the least severe of the three, is a warning letting you know that with enough time and lack of attention, Progress will continue to slow until it comes to a halt.

If you start getting stuck, because the early warning signals are independent of each other, you might be required to address only one of them to help you get back on track to achieving your goal. However, you can also cycle through all three of them if the obstacle you are trying to overcome has multiple levels or is complex enough. As well, know that the first time you are alerted by an early warning signal that it is likely to be a light knock on your door that you are starting to get stuck. However, the longer you ignore it, the louder it will be and the more painful it will be to respond to and resolve.

In my upcoming story about managing my weight, all three early warning signals of stuckness are encountered as my obstacles evolve and I have to escalate my response to address each of them.

The most common scenario is what I refer to as "losing momentum." I think of this as the "I found my objective harder than I thought it would be" perspective. The bad news is that this viewpoint gets in our way of success and happiness often. The good news is that you can call upon plenty of techniques to help you start regaining momentum as soon as you realize you are losing it. For example, several years ago I decided that I needed to lose 20 pounds in order to minimize my constant lower back pain and be healthier. My approach for this was simple—limit my beer intake to facilitate this change (which wasn't much in the first place). Within about 15 days, I was about halfway there (10 of the 20 pounds gone). So, I got excited and celebrated my loss by having dinner and drinks with some friends. After dinner, when I got back home relaxing from the evening, knowing how well my weight loss objective was going, I decided to have a little ice cream (of which I polished off the remainder of the carton). Lo and behold, the next morning, the scale showed 5 pounds higher than my last weigh-in. Frustrated by my lack of self-control, I rededicated myself to staying with my plan. Within a week, and no alcohol, I was back to being halfway to my goal. But surprisingly, I found that I was ready to again "treat myself" for my diligence. Yes, in this example, I was mentally ready, and physically motivated, to bring my weight loss momentum to a halt again and again. I needed some help to keep me focused and avoid the same relapse I had just experienced. Calling upon a simple technique or two from the "What You *Are* Thinking" chapter and reaffirming my goal was all I needed to get me back on track and regaining my momentum again.

Because weight loss is a very complex undertaking, this example allows me to share how techniques might work in the short term, but because new hurdles emerge and new levels of performance are required, you may have to repeatedly escalate your actions to continue to make progress. This brings me to a second scenario of getting stuck; one I call "diminishing returns," whether it happens at a developmental, psychological, physiological level, or all of them combined. You know you are experiencing diminishing returns when you realize even the slightest progress is requiring more and more resources (time, effort, skill, focus, and so forth) to sustain. Using the weight loss example, after about a month, I had dropped 15 of the 20 pounds I set as my goal. I was able to lose this weight by simply cutting out my beer consumption and maintaining that focus for about 6 weeks rather than sabotaging myself every week or two. The problem was that this cut alone had plateaued in its effectiveness and was not going to get me where I wanted to be. A good sign that this early warning signal will start affecting your level of satisfaction is when you determine that doing more of what you have been doing (being tenacious and persistent) won't likely change the outcome. In this case, I couldn't drink less alcohol because I wasn't drinking any, and it didn't matter how long I denied myself because that denial was no longer having any effect. Diminishing returns can be like treading water—while you are likely working hard on your objective, your efforts result in negligible or marginal progress or gain. So, to start making progress again, I considered the techniques found in chapter 6, "What You *Are* Doing," and continued working through the Process until I started seeing improvement again.

Finally is my third scenario where I describe "functional disconnect." With this early warning signal, unlike losing momentum or diminishing returns, most people who are experiencing it are already at a dead stop (or stuck). In this situation, you have uncovered a disconnect between "What You *Are* Thinking" (chapter 5) and your Desire. The disconnect might be in the plan, tactics, or expectations. If you want to allow yourself to achieve the success or happiness you are looking for, you will have to resolve this disconnect. Staying with my weight loss scenario, after cutting my alcohol consumption to zero, I also added a change in diet—more fish, less meat—and added salad to most dinners. At first, I hated the idea of eating salad but I realized that I needed to give a higher priority to my desire of losing weight than I was giving to eating the junk food I loved. It was this reprioritizing (or reweighting) of what was important to me that allowed me to holisti-cally change in my eating habits so that I could move beyond the 15 pounds weight loss wall and achieve the 20 pound loss objective I had set for myself. As a matter of fact, I lost even a little more—something overachievers love to do is beat a goal. Once I beat my goal, I would find myself allowing my desire for junk food to creep in and gain priority almost subconsciously. I would then gain a few pounds, realize what was happening, then lose it again.

As a little insight, I still have a problem with my weight fluctuating (far less than five years ago and in a smaller range variance). I can give you a bunch of juicy rationalizations about the difficulty of maintaining my weight when I travel as much as I do, but that is all they are— rationalizations. When I am home, I maintain my weight or lose the pounds I might have gained on the road. When I am on the road, the longer I am on the road, the more weight I gain. I know exactly what the functional disconnect is. I need to accept the fact that I have to follow the same habits on the road as I do when I am home. But I clearly choose not to, so that says that I have two desires regarding the same issue (to maintain my weight when I am home, and treat myself to comfort food when I am on the road for being away from my family). Balancing my two desires regarding eating and weight loss is only marginally working. The day will come soon enough when I have to finally address this Dr. Jekyll and Mr. Hide situation. I share the example however to show that though I do help others improve their performance using this Process, I am still also a student of it and one who is a work-in-process. However, I have used this Process success-fully in so many aspects of my life to reach new levels of sustained achievement, balance in my life, and focus on what is important. Therefore, I am confident that this book can provide those same benefits to you.

Whether you have lost momentum, are suffering from diminishing returns, or are trapped by a functional disconnect, by determining where you are, where you want to go, and by considering the Process and taking action, you can quickly refocus and start making positive progress again. Understand that, at times, it is probable that you will misdiagnose where you are, or overlook what is really causing you to get stuck in the first place. If you try a Technique and it fails, reassess your situation. Then try several Techniques or apply the Process to see what additional insight those actions provide. Before long, the diagnosis stage will become easier for you, your assessment as to what will likely work will become more accurate, and your recovery time to getting you back on track much shorter.

Why Do We Get Stuck?

We get stuck for two simple reasons. We feel either (1) unsuccessful or (2) unhappy about our progress or priorities. While these feelings can be triggered by losing momentum, diminishing returns or functional disconnect, once you become dissatisfied with how well you are progressing or with your current priorities, you start down the road to getting stuck or being stuck.

What Should "Getting Unstuck" or "Being Stuck" Mean to You?

To address this question, I want to go back to the positive and negative conotations introduced in the Preface, which were:

> *"achieve more success than expected"* and *"achieve results through an excessive, unreasonable, or unwarranted effort."*

Overachievers typically don't have a problem putting in the time and effort to perform at a superior level. Rather, my experience is that they tend to run out of time to address what is important to them because of the excessive effort they are targeting to one or a very few initiatives. This almost single mindedness, maybe even obsessive compulsiveness, can easily allow them to lose sight of balance as well. By overcommitting to one objective, like success with some initiative at work, they might find themselves ignoring their families, health or something else they deem important. Once the overachievers realize the error of their ways, they then put that super-focus on some other aspect of their lives only to find a new imbalance (over-focusing on one objective while sacrificing another) wreaking havoc somewhere else.

If you are one of the overachievers I have been referring to, what I believe "getting unstuck" will mean to you, based on what it has meant to me and the many clients I work with, is that you will be more efficient and effective in how you focus your time and balance your priorities. Staying unstuck is about learning to work *better*, not about learning to work *more* to achieve the objectives you have in mind.

Chapter 2
Desire

Having a desire for something is the first step in the Process. Once you have identified what is important to you, the Desire step then includes creating a plan, plan tactics, a realistic timeline, and reasonable expectations. As I stated earlier, my approach is to immediately start introducing you to a variety of techniques, each followed by a short exercise that will ask you to assess how you are performing as well as how you might apply the technique to help maintain or start building momentum towards your objective. In this chapter, the techniques are focused on helping you discover what you want to achieve. Then, at the end of the chapter, I will integrate what has been covered into a flowchart to help you visualize the Process.

Techniques to Consider as You Begin to Identify Your Desires

Take the Time to Understand What It Is that You Are Really Looking For

One common trap overachievers fall into is raising the expected performance bar long before an objective is reached. As I mentioned earlier, this almost single minded focus to achieve can easily result in allusive and constantly morphing goals. It is like an addiction to perform as we press ourselves harder to achieve, rewriting goals into new ones as soon as we can see the possibility of attainment, all while mentally whipping ourselves with the thought that some form of devastation is looming right around the corner if we even think of letting up.

This reminds me of one of my clients. I started working with his company about 10 years ago. During our first conversation, he told me that if I could help him make $125,000 a year, he would be exactly where he wanted to be. After working with him for less than 18 months, he was making just that amount. Unfortunately, by the time he reached his objective, he had already escalated his goal to a new I-would-be-happy amount which was $250,000 a year. Within another 18 months, he was earning that. But rather than enjoying his incredible success and growth, because he is so driven, he had already fixated on $500,000 annually. Just recently, as we discussed the state of his business, his new I-can-live-with number is about a million a year. The problem is ... when you keep driving yourself, rarely feeling good about where you are and focusing only on where you want to be, you are like a pressure cooker about to explode. He is the perfect example of an overachiever. As he consistently makes progress towards his objectives, he minimizes the value of whatever he has accomplished, and he beats himself up with negative self-talk daily to push himself to perform at a higher level. In the end, while overachievers are often great examples of success, some of them sacrifice everything around them, including their daily happiness, to simply get more of what they already have and are taking for granted.

As you think about the changes you want to make, suppress your urge to attain more long enough to determine if more-of-the-same is what you really want. Regardless of whether my client ever makes an annual salary of a million or not, which I believe he will, unfortunately I don't believe he will find what he is looking for when he does. Why? Because when my client tells me what is important to him, he is clear about what is on that list and money is not at the top of it. So, once you have determined what is important to you—that should be your focus. And if you can't use your time and apply your energy on the highest priority items on your list, that disconnect says that you probably haven't taken enough time to understand what it is that you really want.

Assess yourself on your confidence that you have identified what it is you really want. Circle how you feel you are doing. On this subject, I:

Need a lot of work	Need a little work	Am okay	Feel good where I am

Do you find yourself regularly getting caught up in the chase for "more" of what you are already taking for granted? Have you taken the time to really think through what it is that is important to you and you are focusing on that?

_____

_____

_____

Don't Let the Fear of Missteps and Mistakes Get in Your Way of Determining a Destination

As you will find as you read more, my life sometimes feels—and certainly reads—like a series of missteps. But the way I look at life, those missteps are a big part of what makes me who I am today. Those missteps are what will help me make better decisions tomorrow. By the time you finish reading this book, I hope you embrace the idea that your missteps are not something to be ashamed of, but an integral part of your development and evolution.

I am reminded of a consulting class at the University of Texas in Austin that used one of my books as part of their reading assignments. I came in once a year for several years as a guest lecturer to make some general comments or answer any questions the students might have. I will never forget the time I was sharing some of my experiences in one of the classes, a student raised her hand and asked, very seriously, "Why would anyone ever hire you ... it sounds like all you do is make mistakes." I responded to her, "That is exactly why people hire me .. they want to hire experience. And experience is a short hand word for the phrase 'humbled through failure.'" She wasn't satisfied at all with my answer and quipped under her breath as she sat down, "I wouldn't hire you."

You need to know that defaulting to standards that require mistake-free perfection for yourself will create more problems for you than your performance will ever fix, and unfortunately, overachievers do this a lot. It most certainly will stifle your personal development ability. Your "ability to be correct" percentage can be directly correlated to a timeline. Consider the following figure and the regression curve from the past through the present continuing into the future. The more you are simply making judgments about the past or interpreting results from historical events, the more accurate you can be (hence the phrase "hindsight is 20/20"). For example, with certainty, I can tell you as a CPA how to record a journal entry for a specific transaction that has occurred according to generally accepted accounting principles. However, the more decisions you have to make considering partial data, ambiguous situations, or outcomes in the future, the greater likelihood that you will be wrong. As you move through this timeline, you go from "knowing" to "guessing." In business, the more junior the job function, which usually correlates with lower pay, the more you are expected to know how to do your job because guessing is minimized—most tasks are taught processes, with little room for creativity or variation. The higher the job function, and usually accompanied with higher pay, the more guessing—hopefully informed or educated guessing—is fundamental to the position. Promotions and career advances often come with expectations of becoming more comfortable with ambiguity or the unknown. The more situations like this you encounter, the more likely you will make mistakes along the way. The same progression is true for physical responses as well (but here I refer to it as "familiarity" versus "new"). The more you can call upon your past experiences to perform your current physical requirement, the more successful your attempt will likely be (for example, walking across a narrow log over a creek today calling upon years of practice as a gymnast in your youth). However, when you are in a position where you are trying something truly new with little familiarity regarding that activity to draw upon, your odds of marginal performance are high. This is why setting standards of mistake-free perfection can be so dangerous. This expectation causes us to constantly negatively evaluate our progress therefore pushing us to retreat to the familiar so that we can operate more consistently mistake free at high-levels. By retreating to our comfort zones, rather than allowing ourselves the luxury of failing, we will find it difficult to push the boundaries of our current skills.

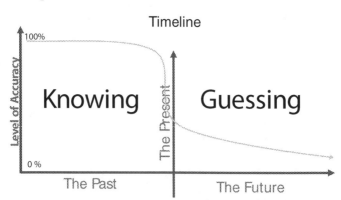

I am bringing this concept up now because I want to make it clear that Desire is not about accuracy or being correct. It is simply about setting your sights on a destination. Mistakes will be made along the way, navigation errors will occur that will unintentionally take you off course. This is predictable and expected. The perspective of "taking every step correctly" will not only impede your forward momentum, but it will likely guarantee that you'll never get there. For example, I clearly remember when I was writing my first book, my wife (also my business partner and a marketing professor at a small Catholic college) would often repeat the same phrase to me that academicians would commonly say, "Don't get it right; get it written." This phrase was coined because when you bog yourself down with the pre-criteria of writing everything perfectly, you will never get anything written. I will augment this saying with "It is far easier to edit something you have already written than to create it in the first place." After you have something written, you can change it, delete parts or all of it, augment it and continue to work on it until you like it. Make your mistakes, edit them (fix them), and keep moving your manuscript forward. Missteps and mistakes are not a sign of failure, but an indication of action, which should be celebrated rather than avoided. It's about progress towards your objective, not about mistake-free perfection in accomplishing it.

Assess yourself on letting the concern for making missteps or mistakes limit your choice of direction. Circle how you feel you are doing. On this subject, I:

Need a lot of work	Need a little work	Am okay	Feel good where I am

What are you trying to "get right" versus "get written?" How are you allowing your fear of missteps and mistakes influence what you are willing to consider as directional choices for your life?

_____

_____

_____

Do the Research, but Learn to Trust Your Gut

As you assess what changes you might want to make in your life, while it is critical that you do your research (contemplation being a major part of that function), at some point "more information" won't add much (diminishing returns) and it will be time to rely on what your gut instincts are telling you. When I refer to gut instincts, I am talking about that feeling you get telling you that something is "right" or "off" when there is little-to-no data supporting that conclusion. I am a big believer in trusting your gut. That is one reason I commonly preface my recommendations to my clients with the phrase, "here are some ideas to consider, but you need to go with what you believe is right for you." So many times with clients, when we get to the point of needing to make an important decision, it becomes time to pull out the pro/con exercise (outlining reasons to do and not to do something). This process generates an outpouring of responses. While this exercise usually starts out noting rational points of view, it doesn't take long for it to shift to emotional perspectives. And somewhere around this point, you see a shift—people start making up reasons or changing the priority of certain ideas to portray a logical imbalance to the pro/con scale so that it starts leaning towards what they are feeling. When I see this, I comment, "If your gut is telling you something—go with it. If it is not working out like you expect, then that is not a problem as we will just make changes along the way."

As you start developing your gut instincts and are learning to rely on them, here is another important lesson to consider. Colin Powell, in one of his leadership speeches years ago, made this point (this was his lesson number 15). He said something like:

> I use the formula P = 40 to 70. Once you have considered between 40% to 70% of the information available, go with your gut (consider that the letter "P" represents probability of success and the numbers following "P" represent the percentage of information acquired as compared to the total available).

As you can see, Colin suggests the information required to make a decision is somewhere between 40%-70%. The first point is clear: do some research. But most of the people I work with would be very uncomfortable thinking they were ready to make a decision with 40% of the information about a subject. And some would feel like 70% of the information was way too low of a bar as well. However, the message simply is, "Don't over-research the choices you want to make." Do a reasonable amount of due diligence and then make a decision. If you are wrong, you will quickly learn from the experience and make whatever course corrections are necessary. If you are right, again you will learn, with the added benefit of reaping the rewards for your accuracy. However, if you continuously research trying to find the definitive answer in an attempt to make the one right decision, you will certainly postpone the rewards you are looking for and you could also miss out on the benefits all together by making your decision too late. Know that all of the research in the world still won't guarantee a "right" decision or that something will work.

As you first start down the road of putting more reliance on what your gut is telling you, recognize that for some, you might have to build it first. If you feel you have already developed good gut instincts, then start leveraging this powerful tool as much as possible. If you haven't, don't worry, just start connecting with that internal feeling that I am calling your "gut instincts" and know that every decision you make from now on—right or wrong—can help you build reliable intuition for successful decision making in the future.

Assess yourself on your comfort in building and listening to your gut. Circle how you feel you are doing. On this subject, I:

Need a lot of work	Need a little work	Am okay	Feel good where I am

What can I do to build more reliable gut instincts? Am I making decisions to quickly, or to slowly based on the research I am doing and what my gut is telling me?

_____

_____

_____

Don't Limit Your Direction Due to Self-Destructive Choices

A common self-destructive tendency I run across is what I refer to as "poor impulse control." Through my experience as a coach, I find that people will often succumb to short term gratification even when it puts at risk what is important to them. For instance, when someone's finances are tight, as soon as that person is starting to feel a little relief from living paycheck to paycheck, he or she might buy new clothes, furniture, or even a new car, which then loads additional financial stress on the situation. Or let's say someone is feeling a little lonely for a couple of days and getting a puppy is deemed to be the fix without serious consideration of the 10–14 year time and energy commitment that is being made. In other words, it is not unusual for us to invoke long-term self-destructive behaviors that derail us from our destination for some momentary escape from our lives.

The stimulation of "new" can feel like a shot of adrenalin, which I have certainly fallen prey to many times. Your new anything can temporarily create a wonderful distraction or fill an empty void. But before you know it, the void or negative emotions that motivated the impulse in the first place will resurface again. There have been numerous research studies over the years supporting this conclusion, which is that "new" generally brings a jolt of energy and or an increase in performance and soon thereafter "new" becomes old and everything reverts back to its previous state.

To be clear, I am not talking about your level of impulse control over whether you buy an extra bag of Cheetos, but rather about ensuring you are managing decisions that have long-term ramifications, especially those that have a high error cost. For example, if you are miserable in your job, impulsively buying a new car to make yourself feel better about the daily commute would be tethering you even more to the paycheck you earn in the job you hate. In this case, the decision to take on significant additional debt or needlessly consume scarce cash reserves would have a high error cost as it could dramatically shrink your available options. As you start working through the task of determining what is important to you, which could take a while before you are ready to make some final decisions, don't dig yourself a deeper hole or severely restrict your flexibility by casually making a few instant gratification self-destructive choices.

Assess yourself on making self-destructive choices limiting your direction. Circle how you feel you are doing. On this subject, I:

Need a lot of work	Need a little work	Am okay	Feel good where I am

What impulse choices are you making that are sabotaging what you really want? What can you stop doing now that will help you more expediently get where you want to go?

_____

_____

_____

Considerations as You Create Your Plan

If You Decide You Want to Make Changes, Know Where You Are Running To

If you decide you want to make some changes, that is great. But before you start running away from whatever it is that you don't like, make sure you know what you are running towards. Consider this scenario: Let's say you are employed by an organization that doesn't allow you to grow or is a demeaning place to work so you want to leave. No problem, just start looking for another place to work. If you are unhappy, don't spend months and years of your life rationalizing that you might as well stay where you are because no matter where you go you won't be treated well: take control of your life and do something about a bad situation!

But I want to provide special emphasis to the phrase "start looking." I didn't just say "quit your job." I said "start looking for another place to work." I don't believe in running away from some aspect of your life, but rather, in running towards whatever change you have decided to make. For example, if you decide you need to develop a new career, before you quit your current job, take time during your evenings and weekends to decide what you want your new career to be. If this means you need to enroll in a school to find out more about some possible choices, then take that step. If you need to change your living situation or get student loans to provide support for your new direction, then do that. I know... if you are in a hostile work environment, you so badly want to tell your current boss to "take this job and shove it" or do an exit interview so that you can tell the company how mismanaged it is. But this craving is only about satisfying your ego, not about changing your direction. For that matter, never burn a bridge unless you have to, which is rare. There was a common saying when I worked for IBM in sales:

> *Love them [speaking about those who directly reported to you] on your way up [your assent into management] because you will need them on your way down.*

Regardless of the change you are contemplating, when you make the decision, be diligent in planning and taking the little steps that will properly position you when it is time to make the jump. When I say, "run toward something," I am proposing that you create a plan, metaphorically start walking first, and as you get in shape (have everything lined up), then start running. Often, what you find by taking this more diligent approach is options open up to you that you might not have ever considered. For example,

- when you prepare to go back to school, you might find that your schedule is such that working part time would not only be possible, but significantly ease your financial burden. Don't be surprised when your current employer gets imaginative and creates a part time position for you (smart business people never let good workers go if they can keep them involved in some way).
- because you kept your job while you were investigating this opportunity, your finances would be in a stronger position when it is finally time to leave.
- you might have found out that there was a minimum of a two year waiting period before you could be accepted into the school of your choice, so continuing to work in your current job ends up providing a great bridge until your opportunity opens up.
- what if you found out during your investigation into possible career changes that your initial idea as to what you wanted to do didn't pan out. In this situation, because you kept your job, you would still have plenty of financial flexibility to start a new search.

My point in this simplistic case study is if someone is unhappy or feeling unsuccessful about some aspect of his or her life, impulsively running from it is not the way to go. However, once that same person decides what he or she wants to do and puts together a plan to get there, now we are talking about running toward the life that you want, which is an approach with an infinitely greater chance for success.

Don't make the mistake of thinking that this technique is just about your work situation. Regularly, people want to run from their circumstances in order to avoid the current pain or frustrations they are feeling. After my dad died, my mom hated her apartment, which was in a very nice retirement home. She hated it because it was where she and dad lived together during his last few years. So, she told me she needed to move and move quickly within a couple months of when he died. We looked at changing apartments, we looked at moving her to a new facility, she stayed with family members for a while to see if that helped her feel better, we considered every idea she came up with and several of those ideas went all the way to the negotiation of a contract or lease. In the end, she realized that she just missed my father and regardless of where she was, she felt the same sense of loss and sadness. Once she realized that she was trying to run from herself, she actually embraced her current apartment and grew to enjoy it even more because it was a reminder of the love they shared together there in his final years.

Before you change your situation, do a self-diagnostic to make sure that *you* are not the cause of dissatisfaction. Don't run away until you know what you are running towards.

Assess yourself on running away. Circle how you feel you are doing. On this subject, I:

| Need a lot of work | Need a little work | Am okay | Feel good where I am |

Is there anything you are or want to run from? If there is, have you decided what you want to run toward or do you just want to run?

_____

_____

_____

Don't Let Inertia Determine Your Direction

Inertia can be like drifting, which actually describes what many people do. What I mean is—many people just do more of what they did yesterday to keep afloat, or robotically attempt the next incremental step forward from where they are right now. It is as if they are treading water working hard throughout life and just letting the current take them wherever it is going. The breakdown in this approach is that it presumes you are exactly where you want to be right now, and that the current is going in the direction you want to go. Overachievers often find themselves in this predicament; working hard treading water going with the current without a clear direction in mind.

Putting a business face on this idea, best-selling author Tom Peters has recommended that companies perform "business process re-engineering" about once out of every five years with "continuous process improvement" during the four years in-between. This is business-speak for make sure you like where you are, you like what you are doing, and you like where you are going about once every five years and then for the 4 years in-between, keep trying to take incremental steps forward.

In my leadership classes, I facilitate a segment on strategy early in the curriculum. I set the stage by sharing thoughts that are articulated in this book and then ask each individual to perform a short exercise. When I first introduce the idea of this self-analysis and vision exercise, I can immediately see the "oh crap" look on almost everyone's faces. This look can best be interpreted as "I hate this touchy-feely stuff and I don't want to waste my time doing it." When they get started though, their attitudes change quickly. During the first few minutes of the exercise, I can almost see each member of the class experiencing a mental, internal battle between the extreme positions of two common personas; the "martyr" and the "self-indulgent." On the martyr side, you have someone who wakes up every day saying, "I may not be chasing the goals I want, but thinking that I have the privilege to manufacture the life of my choosing will only get me in trouble. I have obligations and I just need to buckle down and do what is expected of me." Then you have the self-indulgent perspective, which overachievers commonly squelch on a daily basis. That perspective is one of, "How did I get here? Where do I want to go? Why haven't I been doing exactly what I want? Do I deserve to be able to do what I want?"

Within a very short period of time, people are engaged, writing down their thoughts. And before you know it, my silly, touchy-feely exercise has become a focusing event for many. The reason is simple ... they realized they have been limiting their options as if they only had one possible direction to choose. It is as if we wake up and find ourselves on a set of railroad tracks, and even though we might occasionally struggle with where we are, those tracks allow us to go only forward or backward. So, there we are—stuck on those rails. Then, along comes an exercise that allows you to instantly imagine a new set of tracks going in any direction you choose. It pushes you to imagine that there is a rail switcher immediately ahead. Here is your chance to easily alter the direction you are heading as you will no longer be constrained by the current rails you are riding. Don't be afraid to change directions. Don't let inertia drive your life ... engage the switcher that is dead ahead.

One of my favorite quotes clearly applies here:

> *"Insanity is doing the same things over and over again expecting different results."*

Assess yourself on allowing inertia to drive your life. Circle how you feel you are doing. On this subject, I:

Need a lot of work	Need a little work	Am okay	Feel good where I am

In what important areas have you allowed inertia to drive my direction? What rail switcher directly ahead is it time for me to engage?

_____

_____

_____

Establishing a Clear Direction Provides You With an Essential Sanity Check

Without clear direction, every alternative seems like an opportunity. With direction comes a course of action, whether that is to preserve what you have or achieve something different. Knowing what direction you want to head will drive the creation of a plan. And the greatest benefit of planning is that it provides you with a sanity check to know when you are drifting off course. Regardless of whether we are talking about your personal life, career, or business, I believe it is nearly impossible to get to your desired destination (accomplish your goals) in a straight line. We end up straying from our original course because of mistakes we make along the way, opportunities (detours) we see that we can't pass up, or just having to deal with the chaos that permeates our lives. I think of navigating life as if I were captaining a sailboat. If you start at point A, and are heading toward point B, sailboats have to tack back and forth into the wind to get to the final destination. The trick is not about never veering off course, but to make sure the deviations you make away from your path are not too extreme.

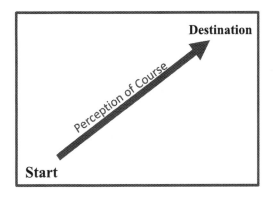

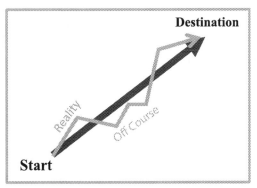

How do you know if you have traveled too far off course? Without understanding your direction, you don't. I remember a client of mine who was in the cable manufacturing business back in the days of memory shortages (we are talking about computer memory in the early 90's, not dementia). This company saw an opportunity to make some quick bucks by speculating in the memory market. And they did. However, the resources they committed to this initiative over the next year, in both cash and the time required by executive management, took them so far off course of their core competency of making computer cables that by the time they refocused their efforts, they had lost an important share of their core market. I see this phenomenon all of the time in business. Should the company do a massive upgrade in technology, should it invest in a new plant, should it re-engineer its production processes, should it revamp the marketing approach, should it create a new product or service offering? I could go on and on with options, but the fact is that every one of these ideas could be the right choice. But choosing all of them simultaneously (or not choosing any of them) is not likely an idea with the best chance of success, because almost all of the world is constrained by resources (time, skill, and money),

> Without a strategy or plan, every option will seem like an equally viable opportunity. And if you try to leverage every opportunity, you probably won't make much headway towards accomplishing any of them.

Once you have pinpointed your direction, you can design a plan to get there. Your plan, the tactics derived from it, a realistic timeline for achievement, the reasonable outcomes expected give you the guidance to filter out options that, while they might seem attractive, are not helping you get closer to your charted destination. It is about focusing on less to get more. It is about making real progress on a few fronts rather than minimal progress on many. You can always change your plan, but until you do, your current plan provides you a critical sanity check to keep you going in the proper direction.

I wasn't always a believer in planning, especially in my personal life. I felt like I didn't need to go through this exercise because I knew roughly what I wanted to achieve, especially in the short term. Besides, it seemed kind of hokey to take the time to write all of it down. So I did a little bit of planning here or there, but nothing consistent or formal. Like so many of my stories, I found myself becoming a believer because my situation, rather than my proactive efforts, dictated a change in my thinking.

In 1991, Michaelle informed me that she wanted to quit her job as a product planner (a lucrative job at IBM bringing products to market) and go back to school to become a professor. She applied to a number of schools and was accepted into the doctoral program at the University of Texas in Arlington, over three hours away from where we lived. The problem was that two years earlier, I had co-founded a new CPA firm with a partner in Austin and Fort Worth, Texas. In Austin, where I worked in an office with three other people, while we were doing well for a start-up, we were not making enough money for me to cover Michaelle's and my finances, living in two cities. However, Michaelle and I have always been supportive of each other's personal growth, so this was not a difficult decision to make. It was simply a decision that would require us to do without for a while. This was especially true when you consider that Michaelle truly did bring home the bacon and fry it up in the pan—she made far more money than I, and did the cooking too. So, to get her to her destination, we created a plan. We looked at the money we were spending and started cutting costs. We sold our country club membership, we kept driving our paid off cars, we leased our house in Austin, and we bought a little place in Arlington, Texas. Additionally, I negotiated with my younger brother and his wife to stay with them during this several year period while I was still working in Austin so that we could make ends meet. With all of these changes, and a little savings, we outlined a way to pull this off for the three years Michaelle needed to be in school.

The original plan was for me to drive up to spend time with Michaelle over a long weekend maybe every other week. At that time, my partners and I were running a typical CPA firm doing tax work, financial statement preparation, and consulting for our small business clients. Almost all of my business came from the local geographic area in and around Austin. Because I predominantly consulted with business owners, the vast majority of my work was performed onsite in my clients' facilities. Therefore, working remotely from Arlington serving my Austin clients was not nearly as reasonable an option as it would be today.

We moved out of the house in Austin, moved everything we could to Arlington (it would not all fit because we downsized), and left a bunch of stuff with various family members. As I drove that large U-Haul truck to Arlington, I realized that this was going to be a long three years as that drive was tedious and boring on a congested highway. I knew I had to find ways to entertain myself given this long round-trip I would be making a couple times a month.

During my first few trips from Austin to Arlington and back, I talked to myself, sang along with the radio and a seemingly endless amount of goofy stuff like this. It was about the third or fourth trip that I realized that this travel time was unique and valuable and I was wasting it. I had a little over three hours each way that was time away from every distraction; time I could put to good use. So I started getting books on tape and allocated half the drive to listening to a new book to learn something new, and the other half to ponder important questions, like "What can I do differently in my business so that I can make more money and spend more time with Michaelle?" This reframing and utilization of my drive-time spawned a number of ideas. Within a couple of months and after beginning to work more closely with my partner in the Fort Worth office, he found some work for me to do there. As well, I came up with the idea to touch base with a nationally known professional education provider to become a speaker and trainer. During these trips, I also came up with a new software product that we immediately started developing which was not only successful, but was sold to a large public company years later. Due to my lack of happiness with my situation with a desire for change, planning became my lifeline ... so I grabbed it. Within three months, instead of working for two weeks in Austin and staying a long weekend with Michaelle, I was able to reverse that situation, spending only two or three days every two weeks in Austin. Within six months, I doubled my income while working mostly out of Arlington. By the end of the year, I had tripled it. With planning came focus. With focus and effort, my life changed. Michaelle and I were able to live in Arlington while she obtained her Ph.D., and except for the first few months, we didn't struggle to make ends meet and really enjoyed our time there (albeit more austere than our life before). Two and a half years after the initial move to Arlington, we packed up and moved back to Austin. While I was still one of the partners in our CPA firm, almost none of my business was in Austin by that time and our firm's clientele was substantially different.

After that experience, we learned the value of having a five-year plan (which we update) and so far in that 20-plus-year period, everything that made the list has been accomplished or completed (with the last item being this book). We don't write a thesis, we simply jot down ideas for individual accomplishment or growth as well as those we want to achieve jointly. We file this away in a folder in a file cabinet and rarely look at it. But in the back of our minds, when that time comes to buy a new car, join a club, or make some investment, we know what to do—whatever supports our plan. Less than a year ago, my wife and I were considering a major remodel of our kitchen and living room. It was beautiful thing to watch as we were grappling with the floor plan. Then, my wife looked at me and said, "Having an updated kitchen and living room would be really nice (we cook often at home), but you have wanted to finish your book (this book) for years. I know you have set aside time to work on it in the next six months, but you know as well as I do that this remodeling project will end up consuming a lot of that earmarked time. The remodel is new to our plan and your book isn't, so let's put the remodel on hold and get this book done now." Michaelle's statement was consistent with so many we both have made to each other over the years ... before committing significant resources, we always look at what is important to us to make sure we are staying true to our priorities. Remember, your plan becomes your sanity check, which keeps you from casually deviating too far off course, but it doesn't lock you into your course either. You can always change or fine-tune your plans. However, because the act of changing your plan requires thought, and sometimes a deep discussion as to what is important, revisiting your plan is a great technique to ensure you maintain positive momentum.

Assess yourself on establishing a clear direction as to what is important to you. Circle how you feel you are doing. On this subject, I:

Need a lot of work	Need a little work	Am okay	Feel good where I am

Have you put together a high-level plan, tactics, timeline and expectations? Are you finding yourself spending time, money and energy doing things that are not that important to you? What is holding you back from coming up with your plan?

_____

_____

_____

Determining Your Desires Should Be an Active Process

I believe that every day, in a way, we do exactly what we want to do or what we Desire. For instance, you might be frustrated by your present weight, but if you don't change your eating habits or exercise regimen, then you clearly do not desire to lose weight.

Another idea that complicates determining what we want, which is far more subtle and complex, is that we subconsciously or consciously suppress many of our Desires. For example, recently, one of my class participants approached me and said, "Bill, I really loved your comments about identifying what you desire and then going after it, but unfortunately, that is not an option for me. I have obligations to my parents and I can't let them down. I wish I could pursue some of the goals that I have in mind, but it is just not possible." Here is what I said after I understood his situation, and I believe the general concept is applicable to many overachievers:

You need to follow whatever your values and beliefs dictate
because I am not trying to tell you what is a right or wrong
choice. However, you also need to understand that you have a
basic obligation to your family and everyone else in your life to
find a way to be happy. If you are not happy, and you feel
trapped by the choices you feel you are being forced to make,
you will eventually take out this frustration on those around
you. And even worse, you might eventually find yourself
repulsed by the people that you are trying to support if you
constantly put their desires before yours, which is the track I
think you are on. Know that when you talk through your desires
with your loved ones, and they share theirs as well, there is a
strong likelihood that you will uncover a good harmonious solution.

For the record, I am happy to say that his life changed within a week
because he confronted his situation with his parents, stopped sup-
pressing his desires, and had several open and frank conversations with
them. As it turned out, his parents were happy to make some adjustments as soon as they realized how frustrated he was. In many
circumstances, we suppress our real desires because we think we are
being selfish to want them.

By the way, there is an important distinction I want to point out as you
give consideration to your Desires. Don't confuse Desire with Wishing.
While wishing and daydreaming usually conjure up ideas for change,
they are not tied to action or accountability on your part to make them
happen. For example, several times a year, my wife will ask me what I
would do differently if we were to win the lottery. While I am happy to
play this mental game, I quickly point out that the statistical odds of
winning the lottery are non-existent if we don't buy lottery tickets. So,
staying with my example, I would use the word "wishing" to describe
someone who wants to win the lottery without buying a ticket, and use
the word "desire" to describe someone who faithfully buys lottery
tickets. To me, wishing is what we do when we want something different, but we are unwilling to 1) take action to change our situation or
2) take responsibility for our role in making the wish come true (effort,
sacrifice, resource allocation, and the like).

Given the pre-work you have done throughout this chapter, I have put
together a summary exercise to help you process this topic more clearly.
Don't spend a lot of time on it ... I just want you to jot down some of
your top-of-mind ideas on the worksheet below. Because there is still
much more to discuss, techniques to introduce, and concepts to
consider, what you list here will likely change some by the time you get
to the end of the book. I have listed Happiness and Success as two different categories for you to consider positioning your mind to think
about. However, they may not be separate to you, or one may be far

more important to you right now than the other. So, fill out what you want and though you are certainly not limited to the space provided here, there is no need to fill in all of the blanks or complete both sections. This is an exercise just for you!

The following statements describe what I want to change or what I want to accomplish so that I can better align how I am spending my limited time and resources to achieve my Desires:

Desires Pertaining to Enhancing My Happiness:

1. _____

_____

2. _____

_____

3. _____

_____

4. _____

_____

5. _____

_____

Desires Pertaining to Enhancing My Success:

1. _____

_____

2. _____

_____

(continued)

3. _____

_____

4. _____

_____

5. _____

_____

Sanity Check

Now for the sanity check. Before you start doing the work (outlined in the next chapter) to achieve any of the goals you have just outlined above, *unless your objective is to get stuck*, you should consider whether you are willing to live with the following statement:

> I am ready to embrace the idea that as I work towards achieving my Desire, I can expect to be required to replan, reprioritize and reaffirm my Desire as part of the normal Process. I understand that the moment my plan is static and unchangeable, the second I take on a rigid perspective on what I think and do, the instant I lock into my current priorities, I will have started down a path to getting stuck or being stuck. Therefore, in order to remain unstuck throughout this effort, when I encounter moments of dissatisfaction, I will simply work through the Process, considering the Techniques outlined in this book so that I can determine what to let go of in order to maintain positive momentum towards whatever objectives I have set for myself.

If you can live with this paragraph, your odds of getting stuck are very small. If you can't, don't worry, I have identified steps to help you get unstuck later in the book. But for now, a more detailed flowchart for the Desire step in my Process can be found on the following page, which I will continue to build upon as we cover more material.

Assuming you have identified something you Desire, have put a plan together that includes tactics, a realistic timeline with reasonable expectations, as well as having a willingness to make the effort to achieve it, you are ready to move on to the next step in this Process—The Work.

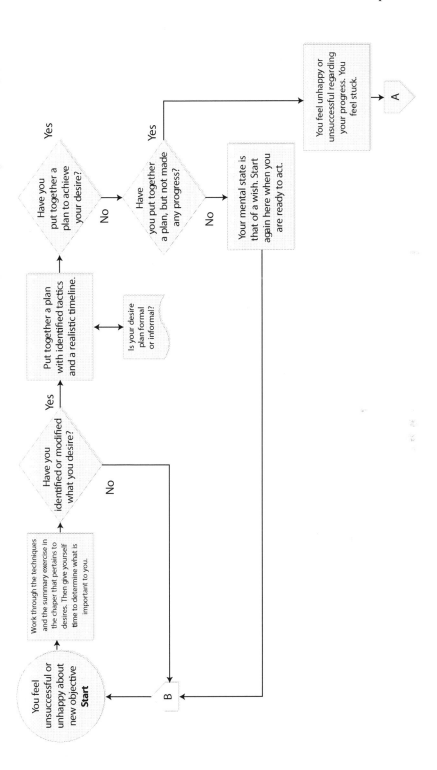

Chapter 3
The Work

Just as I did in chapter 2, I am going to introduce you to a variety of techniques that make up the second step in this Process: The Work. The Work is divided into two sections; the first is about creating a perspective that promotes the work's continuation and the second is about learning how to work "better." While the Desire techniques were created to help you identify what is important to you, the Work techniques are focused on helping you maintaining a consistent sustained self-motivated effort that you can direct towards whatever it is you want to accomplish. At the end of this chapter, I will share an updated flowchart which will include the Work step in this Process.

Sustaining Your Effort and Willingness to Do the Work

The following techniques are covered to help you develop a perspective that will support your ability to sustain your effort and willingness to do the work.

Learn to Appreciate the Joy That Comes From and Surrounds the Work

We spend about 99.7% (statistic totally fabricated but the phrase "vast majority" would certainly apply) of our time en route to some objective. If you can find happiness, serenity, or a feeling of success only when you arrive at your intended destinations, then you are destined to be unhappy or feeling unsuccessful almost all of the time.

I remember my wife and I vacationing in Puerto Rico many years ago. We decided to go to the El Yunque National Forrest Reserve and walk up to the top of one of the El Yunque mountains. Given that we like to hike, this was not a difficult climb because it was only about five miles roundtrip on a paved path. As is typical of my normal overachiever driven self, I focused on getting to the top, pushing myself to walk at a very brisk pace to get there quickly so I could bask in my accomplishment (number of minutes to the top) and the view. Why? Mostly because I am an idiot! I remember Michaelle stopping numerous times and just spending a few moments inhaling the views. The lush scenery, abounding ferns, little tree frogs that made a beautiful unique chirping-like sound, all provided the landscape for this magical stroll. Because I had my head down, digging to keep a constant pace up the grade, I rarely looked at my surroundings. Even when I did look, I thought to myself, "This will be so fantastic when I stop and take it all in at the top." Well, in a little over an hour we finally arrived. At the top, moments before I arrived, cloud cover rolled in. When Michaelle got to the top, because there was nothing there to see, we turned around and started back down. Knowing what I had missed, I was looking forward to absorbing the views as we headed back down. The only problem was those views had also disappeared as the cloud cover was dropping. So rather than being able to take in the gorgeous ten plus miles of views of the land and ocean that I only caught a glimpse of walking up, nothing but a white blanket was visible as far as the eye could see going down.

I can remember that specific moment, which is something for me because I have the memory of a gnat (not so good). As I walked down that trail, I found myself thinking differently. I decided then that I needed to start enjoying where I was and what was right in front of me, and not be blinded by some arbitrary achievement or objective that had to be accomplished before I would allow myself such a luxury. You might conclude that I considered that hike to be a bad experience (certainly it was not for my wife because she enjoyed all of it), but when I changed my perspective, I found myself surrounded by the beauty of that sub-tropical rain forest right there around the path. And though the beauty of the view from the top would have been wonderful, there was plenty to see and hear right in front of me.

You would think that after the El Yunque experience and revelation that I would have this "finding joy in the Work" thing nailed. But oh no, I am a complicated man. It was only a few years ago that I was traveling way too much—one year about 240 days. For many road warriors out there, 240 days away from home would be a piece of cake compared to what they commonly experience, but for me it was way over the line. On one hand, I felt privileged to have the work. On the other, I was not living my plan and my life was out of balance. One particular three month period I was on the road for many weeks, then spent a couple of days at home and then I was off again for another multi-week trip. My schedule was crazy, running from one city to another, one hotel to the next. I was in so many hotels during that period that I couldn't even remember my room number, and when I did, it was often for a room at a previous hotel (you can imagine some of the interesting encounters I had with other guests as they thought I was trying to break into their rooms).

Anyway, during this period, because of my grueling schedule, I often found myself thinking, "If I can just get through Wednesday, I'll be okay" or "If I can just make it through the end of this week, then I will have a chance to relax." I realized as I was getting on a plane one evening that I had successfully wished away several months of my life. Those months of my life were gone and were nothing but a blur. Then I thought if I continued with this lie management strategy of wishing it away rather than enjoying it, I could easily find myself asking "what happened to the last five years of my life?" That night, while sitting on a plane talking on the phone with Michaelle, I remember saying to her, "I am tired, and traveling is not something I want to do right now, but I am no longer willing to 'wish my life away.' I am going to try to stay in the moment and make the most out of whatever I am doing, bad or good. I don't want my life to pass by being only partially engaged by it." Yes, I can hear you grumbling because I thought it too ... "there is nothing wrong with wanting to get through the Work you don't enjoy." I see your point because I have lived it, but I am not buying it anymore.

Wishing time away so that you can get through your Work will cause you to miss a lot of little things that will bring you happiness or feelings of success. Today, when my wife or I see the other completely absorbed by a final goal, we quickly shut that down with our code phrase, "remember El Yunque."

Assess yourself on your attitude towards failure anytime you are doing new work. Circle how you feel you are doing. On this subject, I:

Need a lot of work	Need a little work	Am okay	Feel good where I am

What should you be doing differently to more fully enjoy the work you are engaged in accomplishing? What aspects of the work are you focused on that you commonly find yourself trying to wish away or get through?

_____

_____

_____

Be Realistic Regarding Expectations

During golf season, I like to hit practice balls at the driving range. I also like to take lessons with my golf professional—mostly playing lessons as opposed to ball striking lessons, because just hitting the ball is far less of a problem than the lapse of synapses striking properly in my brain. To clarify, during a normal game, I try to hit shots that I have no business hitting, or forget to stay in the moment, or fail to focus on hitting one shot at a time. But during my playing lessons, I review with the pro what I plan to do and why I am making the shot choices I am proposing. It should be no surprise that with this level of concentration and shot-by-shot focus, I play some of my best golf with my pro in tow.

I remember a specific session a couple of years ago when I was confidently standing over the ball, had a clear picture in my mind of the shot I wanted to make and then just horribly chunked it (I hit more earth than ball). I looked at my pro in embarrassment and said, "I don't understand how I can miss a shot this badly given how much I practice." In his response, Robbin, my pro, recalled a recent teaching event he attended for golf professionals. He commented that when he went out to play 18 holes of golf during this event, he saw Phil Mickelson, one of the best golfers in the world, putting four-foot length putts over and over on the practice green. My pro thought it was odd when he turned the nine and he saw Phil still practicing four-foot putts. And when he completed his 18 holes (a little more than 4 hours from when he started), there was Phil, still practicing those same four-foot putts. My pro was intrigued, so he walked up to Phil and asked him if it was common for him to putt for 4 or 5 hours straight, especially a similar length putt. Phil's comment was something like, "I practice putting four-foot putts for several hours, and when I decide it is time to go home, I have to make 100 in a row before I will allow myself to leave." While this is not an exact quote, it was close enough for me to get the message.

Phil is a pro golfer and one of the best in the world. Putting is a major function within how he makes a living. Yet with all of this practice, for those of us that watch golf, we have all seen Phil miss four-foot putts on tour. So to paraphrase Robbin's response regarding my chunked shot, "What do you expect given that you play golf for fun and only practice a couple of hours a week during a couple of months a year?" To put this into more generic terms:

> *Anytime you have unrealistic expectations given the work you are doing, you are setting yourself up to get stuck because of feeling unsuccessful or unhappy about your performance.*

Assess yourself on your attitude towards failure anytime you are doing new work. Circle how you feel you are doing. On this subject, I:

Need a lot of work	Need a little work	Am okay	Feel good where I am

What am I frustrated with because I am not improving as fast as expected? Where might I be losing momentum doing the work because I am expecting unrealistic gains?

_____

_____

_____

Expect and Embrace Failure Anytime You Do "New Work"

The learning process is often frustrating. So why is it so difficult to learn new things? One answer is that we don't have "hooks" for what we don't know (neither the mental acuity nor the physical skills). An example of this is found anytime businesses train their employees. There is a common misperception that intellectual understanding and skill development are the same. I see people regularly giving instruction to their direct reports and then walking away thinking that the employee is now capable of competently completing a task or project just because it was explained verbally. If an employee has successfully done this work before, and the explanation is simply a reminder of the steps and processes to be followed, then success is likely. However, most of the time, the person receiving the instruction is being bombarded with a combination of previously known and new information simultaneously. When this occurs, especially regarding the new information, most of it will likely come across like a fire hose shooting water—a stream of information splashing everywhere. Except in rare circumstances, a high volume of splashing information does not change one's ability to perform. In order for our skills to improve, we typically need to go through a "Learn, Try, Fail™" cycle that looks like this:

- First, we need an intellectual understanding of wat we are trying to accomplish.
- Second, we need to experience what we just learned.
- Third, based on that experience, with the likelihood of failure being some part of that experience, we can then discover

important gaps in our understanding that negatively impacted our performance, and ask for updated information.

- Fourth, repeat steps two and three until we are fully competent to do the work without supervision or guidance.

As we perform steps two and three over and over in the "Learn, Try, Fail™" cycle, we are repetitively building new "hooks" to hang new information or skill upon.

Let me digress for a moment to better conceptualize this "hooks" idea. Picture a big coat closet full of hooks screwed on the wall. In this scenario, hooks represent our brain's access system to whatever is hanging in the closet, and coats represent information, experience, or a combination of both that we want to access. Some of the hooks in the closet will have heavy coats hanging on them, others light coats, and some no coats at all. Additionally, picture a lot of room for new hooks to be screwed into the wall when more are needed. Now consider something as mundane as improving your skills using Microsoft Word™. First, in order to teach someone how to use this program, as I noted above, you need to provide both an intellectual understanding of what to do as well as the opportunity to experience doing it. So, if I were to teach a class on this subject, I would want to explain the material in sections (chunking or learning in chunks) and then have each person perform specific tasks on their own to cement-in that learning before moving on. Why? Because in working through this cycle, the trainee will identify what he or she *did* and *did not* understand. Each time someone identifies what is not understood, awareness starts to generate a new hook to store more information. If there was already some knowledge or comfort with the information just covered, then think of that situation as a hook being in place with only a windbreaker on it (some awareness of the topic, but needing more for a greater understanding and applicability). The more that person learns, or the better skilled the person becomes, the more that wind-breaker turns into a heavy coat full of knowledge and expertise.

Repetition is the fastest way to generate new hooks. We need to experience and re-experience what we have been learning, which will produce new hooks that will allow us to hang our developing knowledge and skill (coats). Without hooks, the coats simply end up on the floor. And while the information may be in the coat closet, we have no easy way to retrieve it or build on it.

Most organizations simply provide the planning or intellectual component of the training process. Management tells people what to do and what steps to follow. Even if they are conveying that information in the right amount of detail, the problem is that they mistake the transmission of facts and data with the recipient's ability to be able to assimilate it and do it. The recipient might have heard it all, even taken good notes, but if there are no available open hooks, all that new information will just be lying on the coat closet floor. We typically jump to the erroneous conclusion that the recipient's successful assimilation of the new plan and knowledge equates to skill development (for example, I can watch a specific martial arts technique and understand it, yet not be capable of performing it). We need to know what we are trying to do, attempt it, evaluate what we did grasp, identify what we missed, and then repeat over and over. With each progression of the Learn, Try, Fail™ cycle, we combine a little more knowledge and experience to create a little more skill. Don't short yourself by losing sight of this important cycle. Put in the time to build the hooks you need in order to continue progressing towards whatever you are trying to achieve.

Assess yourself on your attitude towards failure anytime you are doing new work. Circle how you feel you are doing. On this subject, I:

Need a lot of work	Need a little work	Am okay	Feel good where I am

Where can I apply the Learn, Try, Fail cycle to help me achieve my objectives? How do I need to restructure my personal training, as well as the training of others, to incorporate the idea of building more open hooks to improve the overall development process?

_____

_____

_____

What to Stop Doing Is Often More Important Than What You Are Doing

As you continue doing the work, as you make progress towards your desires, much of your focus should rightfully be on "What can I do today to move me one step closer to whatever I am trying to achieve?" While "doing the work" really seems to be about actions you should take, often it is just as much—if not more—about what actions to *stop*.

In martial arts, regardless of the activity, learning to use proper technique is essential. Recently, John has been breaking down complex movements and coupling them with verbal mnemonics to help his students understand exactly what he wants them to do, and not to do. While I often don't have difficulty executing various techniques, I almost always have a problem performing the techniques properly. For instance, I might incorporate extra strength into the movement to offset the fact that I was only partially correctly utilizing the technique being taught (which didn't require strength, but rather leverage or flow). So, when I am doing the work, I need to remember that my first priority is to learn the technique, not to execute it. I have to stop trying to be someone who can quickly mimic the technique in order to be the person who has correctly learned the technique.

Managing what "not-to-do" shows up in every objective you set for yourself. A few months ago while I was skiing, I was clumsily traversing downhill after 9 months of being away and had to remind myself to stop leaning back in my boots so that I could turn more easily and quickly. Recently, when I was juggling about 10 business projects at the same time, I had to stop reacting to whoever was screaming the loudest and start working off my "what-is-the-best-use-of-my-time-now" to-do list so that I could get more done in a shorter period of time rather than spinning in circles because I was constantly jumping from project to project. One night in the last few weeks, I found myself in bed trying to go to sleep while I was visualizing a challenge over and over in my mind. I knew that if I didn't stop the circus going on in my head I wouldn't be refreshed enough to properly deal with my situation in the morning. Today, while I was working on this section of the book, I had to stop being judgmental about what I was writing and let my thoughts flow freely knowing that later I could fine tune what I had written. It doesn't matter what you are doing, for every step forward you want to take, progress is often predicated as much or more on stopping something you are doing as it is about starting something.

As you consider starting or stopping an action, recognize that whatever you decide to do, you need to approach it in a sustainable way. This is one of the major change management points I review with my clients regularly. Working with one of my CPA firm clients recently, it was decided that all of the partners needed to start spending more time in front of their clients. The client identified that this action would not only create greater loyalty, but was a best practice in the profession as well. Due to hearing frequently what was keeping their clients awake at night, the partners would improve the odds of being asked to do additional work, increase the possibility of referrals from those same clients, and be positioned to provide higher-valued services given their enhanced knowledge. After this decision was made, the group decided that each partner would be required to set up at least one meeting a week with existing clients. They also decided to track these appointments to make sure everyone was living up to expectations. Then, at their monthly meetings, they planned on sharing their experiences to put peer pressure on partners who were falling short of expectations, as well as penalize them financially for their under-performance. To be fair, I supported every step in this initiative except one: the once a week requirement. I suggested they start off scheduling these "gain aware-ness" client meetings once a month for each partner for the first six months and then start increasing the frequency once the success of the initiative was clear to everyone.

For many who read this, the idea of requiring only one client visit per partner per month could be viewed as an almost meaningless effort. "Why even bother?" you might be asking. Well, remember the idea of sustainability. At that time, only a few partners in that firm made these kinds of visits and they were sporadic. Under this new plan, visits would be required of every partner and tied to financial rewards or punishments. Given that the partners already had their plates full with work, the firm needed to recognize that it was going to get some pushback because partners were being asked to trade effort that was comfortable (doing project work) for an effort that was uncomfortable (visiting clients in more of an advisory role). My suggestion of one visit per month was not based on magic. I knew from experience that while a member or two of the group might achieve four visits per month consistently over a several month period, the likelihood was that the majority would not get there. Sure enough, after the first month, one of ten partners made the required visits. After the second month, a dif-ferent partner of the ten made the required visits; but still only one partner met the requirement. At the end of the first quarter, this initia-tive was scrapped because everyone was failing at it. It wasn't abandoned because it was a bad idea ... it was ditched because we tried to force change at a pace that the partners were not ready to sustain. In this situation, for this new expectation to have gotten legs, we would have needed 7 or 8 of the 10 partners to be successfully fulfilling the new requirements every month. A high compliance rate like this would have started changing the culture and putting pressure on the few outliers rather than the way it actually worked with low compliance and abandonment.

Coming full circle to integrate the examples in this section, real change often comes from small sustainable actions that pool together creating magnitude over time and progress comes as much from what you stop doing as it does from what you are doing.

Assess yourself as to your success at keeping top of mind both what to start and stop doing. Circle how you feel you are doing. On this subject, I:

| Need a lot of work | Need a little work | Am okay | Feel good where I am |

Are you staying focused as to what to stop doing that can help you achieve your objectives? Are you approaching what you do and don't do in a sustainable way?

_____

_____

_____

Learning to Work "Better" Instead of "Harder"

Overachievers typically don't have a problem working hard, but they often have a problem working "better." So, that is the focus of this section—learning how to work better. Regarding any technique, know that by remaining open to learning while doing the work (letting go of what you think you know), that is where you will find the "wisdom in the work," which can bubble up into profound thoughts and ideas that can help you work better.

Balance Short-Term Efficiency Gains Against Long-Term Effectiveness Expectations

It is important to be aware of the choices you make every day between being effective and efficient in your performance. In my view, being effective implies taking the necessary steps to achieve your desired long-term results. Being efficient is about managing short-term waste—focusing on the fastest way to get results. The idea of working better is based on being both efficient and effective in what you do. But all too often, we take the gains available from short-term efficiency while putting at risk or sacrificing our long-term effectiveness.

When I joined my current martial arts school about 14 years ago, because of my 8 years of previous training in "hard" martial arts styles, I quickly advanced in rank (when you join a new school, you start over as a white belt). I shied away from the "softer" Chinese and Japanese styles taught at the school because I felt that I could get promoted more quickly building on what I already knew (efficient). The problem was by the time I was a purple belt (a beginning instructor level), I was way behind in my overall development toward becoming a black belt because of my limited knowledge of the softer side of martial arts. After I realized the error of my ways, I started focusing on the Chinese and Japanese styles. But learning how to be softer at this point of my development was even more difficult because not only did I have to learn new skills, I had to unlearn many bad habits I had developed over the years by over-committing to the harder styles. I chose the short-term gain in performance (efficiency) over making important long-term progress (effectiveness) towards my overall objective. In the end, what seemed like a shorter path to black belt actually became a much longer one.

Consider my earlier discussion regarding training your people as another example of this technique. The most efficient approach we can take to maximize the production of our people is to tell them to do only those projects they (1) currently know how to do, (2) can do without supervision and (3) can complete with no mistakes. For today, tomorrow, this week, and maybe this month, the company will reap rewards for this philosophy. During the short term, why train anyone to be better, faster, and stronger when we can get more out of those people by having them produce at their maximum capacity right now based on what they already know and have been successfully demonstrating? So, a common question on the table for my clients is, "should we focus on gaining more production and rewards now, or should we focus on building a stronger more profitable organization for the future?" My response is "balance"; we need a certain level of production to be profitable now, but we also need to be building a workforce that is competitive and profitable in the future.

This brings me to another concept, which is:

We too often allow the urgent to take priority over the important.

When we focus on the urgent, we tend to make short-term efficiency choices. Working better is about incorporating the power of both efficiency and effectiveness, not about sacrificing one for the other.

Assess yourself as to whether you commonly sacrifice long-term effectiveness for short-term gains or efficiency. Circle how you feel you are doing. On this subject, I:

| Need a lot of work | Need a little work | Am okay | Feel good where I am |

Where might I be sacrificing long-term effectiveness for short-term efficiency gains? How can I work "better" so that my efforts are both efficient and effective?

_____

_____

_____

Continually Evolve Your Skills and Abilities

John teaches us that there is a hierarchy to learning martial arts. First you learn techniques, like punching and kicking. As you gain confidence in your technique, you can jump to a higher level and incorporate interval into your self-defense toolkit. Interval is just like it sounds—an awareness of the role distance plays in an encounter. For example, if you find yourself in a fight with someone much taller than you, your best chance of defending yourself, assuming you and your opponent have similar abilities, is to move in close, strike, and then immediately get back out of range and do this over and over. Why? If you are at an improper distance, because of your opponent's much longer arms and legs, he or she will be able to hit you from a distance that you can't hit back.

As you incorporate interval into your thinking, timing becomes the next level to consider. Timing is "the when" to do something. It is not about constantly throwing kicks and punches, but throwing them when your opponent is presenting you with opportunity or is vulnerable. From this point, breathing is the next higher level. Though you may have good technique, well managed interval to protect yourself, and effective timing, without good control of your breathing, you won't last more than about 60 seconds in an engagement. Once you are exhausted, even great skills won't be of much value to you if you are too tired to respond to your opponent. Therefore, having a greater awareness of your breathing and accessing techniques to control it is the fourth level of development. Finally, the fifth and highest level is "mind." Operating at this level is about managing your physical, emotional and mental states in order to stay calm, focused, in the moment and positioned to deliver the best of what you have to offer. Mind is also about a state of consciousness that allows you to see and feel when your opponent is about to do something, sometimes even before the opponent knows he or she is going to do it.

I can apply John's developmental model to the business world in a couple of different ways. The first exactly follows his martial arts version. Technique is your technical skill. When you have developed your technical skill to a certain level, you can continue to develop it, but you need to augment that learning with Interval. I equate interval in business to maintaining the right distance between people. At this level, how you work with, manage, lead, and influence others takes the spotlight. This is about the human side of doing your job and learning to work through others rather than just doing everything yourself. Next is timing. This one is simple to explain, but difficult to pull off (and not without some element of luck). Every business owner that I have worked with that has become extremely successful knows that while they worked hard, their success was partially attributed to timing—they offered their product or services at the right time and the right place. In short, becoming more aware of how timing affects success and how to leverage market momentum takes your skills to a new level.

Breathing is next, and I think it is the same for both martial arts and business. Controlling your breath, staying relaxed, and maintaining your stamina is how I interpret this stage. Finally, we move to the big Kahuna: mind. Just like in martial arts, it is about managing your physical, emotional and mental states. It is about developing the emotional intelligence to interpret how you are feeling and also manage yourself in a way that others can't determine what is going on inside you. It includes the ability not only to become aware of the concerns and emotions of others, but to be able to use that knowledge and empathy to manage them through influence and leadership.

The entrepreneurial type (which I am one) reminds me of another variation of the need to evolve to the next level. Entrepreneurs commonly

- are willing to take risks,
- have hundreds of what they consider great ideas,
- believe almost solely in their own judgment,
- are optimistic, and
- are passionate about what they are doing.

I can go on and on about their wonderful qualities, but I know you get the picture. Entrepreneurs are fantastic at starting businesses and building them to a certain level of success. However, in many cases, they are also their own worst enemy because those same qualities that make them great at developing something out of nothing tend to stall them out when they are trying to make something into more. When I coach these business owners, it takes every ounce of my energy, and sometimes that still isn't enough, to get them to focus and stay with one or two of their best ideas until they give them a chance to work. By the time these people get half-way into an implementation plan with one idea, they have come up with a better idea that needs to take its place. They simply get bored managing the day to day tedious stuff and love whatever they have conjured up that is newer and more exciting. It is very difficult to get entrepreneurs to implement systems and processes because they feel this kind of infrastructure is stifling.

What I have found when I get involved with very profitable and growing businesses is that they often achieve that success because of entrepreneurs who create the vision and continually evolve products and services that are of interest to the market. But at the same time, those same businesses will also have someone else (I refer to them as operators) who are highly respected and in an equally strong positions that appreciate processes, procedures, systems, and consistency. The best way I can say this is

> Without the entrepreneur, there would be no business. But if the entrepreneur can't evolve his or her skills to another level and embrace the characteristics of an operator, his or her business will likely top out long before its potential is realized.

Some entrepreneurs, although few, can shed their skin and morph into operators when necessary. This, when it occurs, is the best example I can give you of someone evolving to another level. To be clear, as that same business grows and gains even greater success, at some point the operator mindset will reach a ceiling as to its benefit and the operator will have to give way to another level or different approach to running and sustaining the business. In other words, we all need to recognize that the skills that make us successful won't keep us successful. A book by Marshall Goldsmith has a title that encapsulates this thought best, called: *What Got You Here Won't Get You There: How Successful People Become Even More Successful*. This is a difficult message for most to believe. Why would anyone abandon what has been working for them and replace it with an approach that is not only foreign to them, but is unproven as well? Usually they don't, which is why many small businesses remain small businesses. But there are also plenty of executives that continue to drive their organizations to new heights because they understand that while change can be risky, remaining the same can even be riskier.

Finally, evolving your skills and abilities to the next level can also be a function of making sure you have access to a variety of tools, and are always trying to use the right tool in your toolkit for the project at hand. It's the old adage, "If the only tool you have is a hammer, everything will look like a nail." While applying a single tool to every situation might often work, it certainly does not fit the idea of working better, but rather one of working harder.

Learning to work better often comes down to knowing when your work approach or your over-reliance on a skill is showing diminishing returns or starting to be less effective. By having a greater awareness and acceptance of the need to continually evolve your skills and abilities to the next level, you will likely not only be more open to doing things differently, but more willing to do different things.

Assess yourself on continuing to work to evolve your skills and abilities. Circle how you feel you are doing. On this subject, I:

Need a lot of work	Need a little work	Am okay	Feel good where I am

What can I do to evolve on every level, from technique, to interval, to timing, to breathing, to mind? What should I be doing to incorporate different tools in my toolkit or finding new approaches that can allow me to work better?

_____

_____

_____

Changing Your Plan When Doing the Work Is Not Only Okay, but Expected

This sounds like an odd comment to make given the importance I have assigned to identifying your desires and creating plans and tactics to achieve them. But we aren't focusing on Desire in this step, but rather the Work needed to achieve your desires. Desires and plans change, or we need to be flexible enough to allow them to change as we gain more knowledge, skills, or experience as we do the work. In other words, you want to leverage the wisdom you gain from doing the work. When we start out attempting to achieve our various objectives, understand that "we don't know what we don't know." And because planning is the first step in this Process, it is easy to see why creating a plan when we don't know very much can easily produce the need for change along the way. People often find comfort in having a plan, and this causes them to put on blinders, continuing to carry out the identified tactics, regardless of the changes going on around them. When plans or tactics are set in stone, they can not only shift from being a strength to a weakness, but can actually become worse than having no plan at all.

Consider my example in chapter 1 of a sailboat going from destination A to B. Let's say island C is closer but a little less desirable, which is why the original plan was to head toward island B. Now assume you have set sail for island B and are more than halfway there. Out of nowhere comes a coast guard alert that a terrible unexpected storm is rolling in fast; a storm that would make it impossible to navigate, could damage the boat and even jeopardize lives. Clearly, this storm wasn't part of the plan or expected. You are closer to island B than returning to island A, but island C is significantly closer than either. So, given this scenario, locking into island B as your destination would be a bad choice, especially since island C is much closer and safer. As new information is unveiled, especially when it is significant (like in this weather scenario), your current plan and tactics should be revisited and course corrections made to take advantage, or minimize the damage, of what the new circumstances may bring. Remember what I said earlier about planning:

> Plans are a great sanity check. They help you decide whether the considered course alteration will support achieving your plan, or whether the Desire or plan needs to be revised due to the importance of the course alteration.

Sometimes overachievers confuse planning with reaching the top or the pinnacle. In other words, we make planning about achieving something, like ascending to the top of El Yunque or reaching island B, because that is what we decided to do. In reality, getting to island B or the top of El Yunque was probably more of a tactic in the overall plan to "have fun, get some exercise, enjoy the outdoors," and so on. Don't get too committed to your plans or tactics as they need to remain flexible. Even though island C was not the preferred destination, given the weather circumstances outlined, it quickly became the best tactic to reach the broader goal of enjoying the day. Taking this scenario a step further, while enjoying the day was the original broader goal when you set sail, my guess is that it quickly lost priority to an even greater desire to remain safe. The change in course direction to island C is a perfect example of how time, new information, greater insight, and the like can instantly motivate you to reprioritize your desire. As you can see, locking into your plan can be dangerous.

As I think about inappropriately locking into my plans, I remember the first software product I started designing and writing for my own use and resale. It was a point of sale system for my ladies' clothing stores. The software created was basic, but so was our business. This was more than 30 years ago and there was not much on the market that was economically reasonable, especially for a small business like ours. We then opened our second ladies' clothing store, and soon after, bought a franchise called Software City out of Teaneck, New Jersey. Among the three businesses, we had a number of needs that were not being addressed by our simple program, so it was time to rewrite it. By this time, I had a partner who was a brilliant programmer. So, we established the goal of designing and developing a point of sale system that would not only handle our three stores, but every one of my retail clients' operations too. We locked into our plan to create the most versatile point of sale system we could imagine and no matter how complex it became, or how much time it took to add all of the features we could envision, we were going to get this done right. We made it so flexible and robust that it became too complicated to set up and use.

During our four-year prolonged development approach, many other software products were released in the market that were vertical in nature, catering only to specific types of businesses instead of trying to respond to everyone in retail like we were trying to do. To make a long story short, we ended up selling this product to one of our clients for use in their one-hundred stores. The market opportunity for our point of sale system had severely diminished because we had locked into our original plan. We were going to get to island B no matter what storms were brewing, regardless of the resources it was requiring, or how much risk we were going to encounter. The good news is that we did learn our lesson from this, although we were pretty beaten up by it. The next product we developed was an e-learning viewer (Professional Automated Self Study, or PASS) that helped convert text materials quickly into self-study courseware. When we took on this project, based on what we learned from our point of sale product development experience, we decided to build releases of the product in six-month intervals or less. With this approach, we got the product to market very quickly, received timely feedback that helped make the offering more desirable, and we started making money right away. This was a far more successful approach because our plans took less time to execute and we modified those plans instantly with the marketplace feedback we got earlier and often.

There are two messages here. The first is that sometimes your desire includes everything you can dream of in one giant step, which might take a decade or more to achieve. While you absolutely want to keep the grandiose in mind, think about setting milestones along the way with shorter horizons for completion and reassessment. This way, you can test out whether the changes you are making are really moving you closer to what is important to you. With each milestone you pass, you also gain perspective as to whether what you thought you wanted is what you actually want. Second, make the planning process about responding quickly and leveraging what you learn along the way, and know that changes to your desire, plan, plan tactics, timelines and expectations is not only okay, but expected.

Assess yourself as to whether you are currently locking into one of your plans. Circle how you feel you are doing. On this subject, I:

| Need a lot of work | Need a little work | Am okay | Feel good where I am |

Regarding my objectives, where am I locking into my desire, plan, plan tactics, timeline or expectations that are positioning me to work harder rather than better? How can I keep at the top of mind my broader desire so that I don't get overly committed to a plan or a tactic within that plan?

_____

_____

_____

Recognize That You May Be the Obstacle You Have to Overcome

A couple of years ago, when I was consulting onsite with the executive team, one of the managers pulled me aside and asked me for some personal advice. She said, "I am thinking about asking to go part-time because the stress of this job is really getting to me. What do you think they will say?" I told her that I thought they would be willing to do whatever she wanted. But then I added, "What are the owners or your direct boss doing to create this stress?" Here was the conversation that followed:

> **Manager:** "There is so much work for me to do and I just can't get it all done. Every day, they pile more things on my plate and I just can't keep up. This overload has started to impact my home life and I am concerned that it is only going to get worse."

> **Bill:** "What has management been saying to you? Have they been complaining that you are not able to get everything done? Are they pressuring you to stay late and get the work out? Please describe to me what is going on."

> **Manager:** "It is not that. The management team, and my direct boss the CEO, has been wonderful. They all tell me to get done what I can, and if I need help, to let them know."

> **Bill:** "I am confused then. What is the problem?"

> **Manager:** "I know this stuff needs to get done, and I worry about the fact that it isn't. I know it is important or they

wouldn't ask me to do it. I feel like I am letting them down. As well, I really can't relax as long as I have an inbox full of work to do."

Bill: "So, please explain to me how going part-time will help your situation? It seems to me that since you can't do everything on a full-time basis that you certainly won't be able to get it all done on a part-time one."

Manager: "Well, I was thinking that if I went part-time, they would not expect me to do as much and that would take a lot of pressure off me."

Bill: "But you already told me that *they* were not putting pressure on you in the first place. What you said was that *you* felt like you were letting them down and that *you* can't relax as long as you have an inbox full of work. I am sorry to point this out, but *you* are the only problem you have here. Until you stop beating yourself up for ridiculous expectations as to how much you should be accomplishing, and you learn to relax when your inbox is full, nothing will change."

Manager: "Okay ... I hear you. So you are suggesting that I don't go part-time, but rather, that I quit all together?"

Bill: "No, I am not saying that at all."

Manager: "Well, if I quit, then I won't worry about letting them down and the inbox issue goes away."

Bill: "Yes, your statement is true about working here. But whatever you choose to do with your life, whether that is work for someone else, work for yourself, or choosing to do some charitable work, you will always find someone you don't want to disappoint. Based on my experience with you in the past, this is about you caring about what you do and how you are perceived, not about anything anyone is doing to you. And while quitting may ease your pain for the next month or two, you will likely just rebuild this exact situation in short-order again where ever you go. When you run from yourself, you quickly find there is no place to hide! You simply have to give yourself permission to do what you can, and let go of what you can't. Each day, calm yourself in the face of chaos, quit beating yourself for not being superwoman, know that it is a rare luxury when your inbox will actually be empty, and learn to relax and enjoy what you are doing while finding comfort in whatever progress you are making."

This type of conversation doesn't just happen once in a while; it happens often. It is not uncommon for overachievers to blame others, situations, and environments for making us feel a certain way, when in fact, the only problem we have is with the way we think. It is important for you to recognize the possibility, and even the probability, that at some point you will become the greatest obstacle to achieving your goals. Be ready to change the way you work, the way you respond, the approaches you take and the way you think so that you are poised to work better rather than just continuing to work more.

Assess yourself as to whether you are the obstacle you have to overcome to achieve your objective. Circle how you feel you are doing. On this subject, I:

Need a lot of work	Need a little work	Am okay	Feel good where I am

What am I doing right now where I am the biggest hurdle I have to overcome to achieve my objective? What can I do to recognize early-on when I am putting myself in my own way?

_____

_____

_____

Take What's Given

In the practice of martial arts, this concept is drilled in to teach us to respond to what our opponent is offering rather than either following some mental plan we have conjured up or over-relying on our strengths. When you have an unfamiliar opponent, both a mental plan and leveraging strengths require information you don't have to dependably work. In other words, those two options presume superiority; that I know my strengths are greater or that my plan has all the necessary contingencies to appropriately react to the actions and reactions of my opponent. How could you have this level of knowledge or insight about an unknown opponent? So, to give yourself the best chance of securing the outcome you are looking to achieve, it is important to continually respond to whatever opportunities or weaknesses your opponent is offering to you. John refers to this interactive response to openings as they become available as "Taking What's Given."

This technique is powerful and can be easily applied to any aspect of your life. For example, when I was restarting my consulting practice about a decade ago, my wife and I went for a walk. Our walk included one of those all-too-common enlightening sessions where she held a philosophical mirror to my face and said, "Why aren't you listening to your own advice?" Here was the situation.

Just before this period, I had taken a couple of years away from my practice to work for one of my clients to help them with their start-up dot-com. As I restarted my practice, I was receiving a number of phone calls from CPA firms asking me to provide them with practice management assistance. Though I had worked with a number of CPA firms in the past, other professional service organizations and family businesses were equally part of my client mix. The call volume continued to accelerate on the CPA firm side, but I did very little to look for that type of work or even less to attract it. My plan was to rebuild the family business side first even though that marketplace was slower to respond to my return. Then came the walk with Michaelle. She asked me, "Why aren't you more aggressively pursuing providing services to CPA firms since that profession seems to be constantly knocking at your door right now?" I replied boldly, "Because I don't see myself specializing as a CPA firm practice management consultant!" She replied, "Apparently that is not the case because that work represents the last four or five projects you have done." And then she said, "Why are you fighting this? You always talk about 'take what is given,' yet you are clearly not following your own advice."

By the end of our walk and from the clarity of our conversation, I had decided that it was time to proclaim that one of my specialty areas of work was CPA firm practice management consulting and I started putting market efforts behind that message immediately. Within two years, my consulting business was more successful and profitable than it ever had been before. As you know from my bio, I have received honors such as being named one of the most influential CPAs in the profession, have been listed as one of the top 10 CPA firm consultants to the profession, selected as an ambassador for the profession, and much more. The point is ... I had opportunity all around me, but I was looking for something specific rather than opening my eyes to what was right in front of me. Fortunately, Michaelle was there to guide me to the opportunity that I was refusing to see.

"Take What Is Given" is a technique that can quickly help you work better and find greater success and happiness because it is all about leveraging the support, momentum and opportunities being presented to you. All you have to do to take advantage is to stop fighting it.

Assess yourself as to whether you regularly are taking what is given. Circle how you feel you are doing. On this subject, I:

| Need a lot of work | Need a little work | Am okay | Feel good where I am |

Where might I be ignoring the opportunities being presented all around me because I am looking for something specific rather than taking what is given? What can I do to more frequently and easily see what is being given?

_____

_____

_____

Always Keep the Basics Top of Mind (Constantly Build on Foundational Areas)

I introduced this concept in the preface, but I am covering it now in more detail to show how it can help you work better. This technique is about making sure you are always building on a strong foundation—strong enough for where you are now, but also strong enough to support where you plan to be. If your foundation isn't built for the load you will eventually put to bear on it, then though you might make great progress doing the work in the short term, your gains will all crumble underneath you in the long term. Think of Tiger Woods. At multiple points in his career thus far, even though he was the world's number one golfer, he chose to rebuild his swing. Why would anyone change a swing that was ranked as being the best in the world? It had to be because he aspired to do more and felt like he had gotten all that he could out of his existing foundation. So he has decided multiple times to rebuild on a new one which would support future pressure and success as he aged and changed.

"Foundation" is the most frequently mentioned directive at John's school. John and his instructors might say the mantra "feet, center, and martial intent" about every 10 minutes in class to remind the students to continually focus on building a strong foundation before they start micro-focusing on other movements. Here is a quick explanation of the mantra:

Feet: Make sure you feel your feet throughout every movement, and in every phase of a movement. For example, with a punch, it should originate from the ground, through your feet, into your legs, through your trunk, into your limbs to your fists. Every action starts with energy generated from pushing off the ground rippling through your body until it reaches its intended target.

Center: Move from your center, take deep stances, maintain a low center of gravity and stay in balance. Don't initiate movements by learning forward or backward—start them from your belly. Keep your shoulders back and relaxed with your butt rolled under so that your body is in a strong upright position. This culminates in a strong balanced posture with your body positioned to dynamically react and respond in any direction.

Martial Intent: Whether you execute a strike, block, avoid, grab, kick, or any other, technique, do it as if you have an opponent. Or another way to say this is ... with any response you make, always have a target in mind.

"Back to the basics": This four word phrase transcends, at least at John's school, all his martial arts teachings. Whether the style is hard or soft, at a distance or body-to-body, offensive or defensive, these words provide the foundation upon which every technique is built. It is a constant reminder that your skills under pressure will likely crumble if you don't take this long-term foundation-building development approach.

This mantra is easily applied, and helpful, regardless of the task at hand, whether my focus is on my life, my business, a sport I am playing, or any other endeavor in which technique is important. For example, as a golfer, I apply this principle every time I address a golf ball. I think about making sure I can feel my feet ... the center through the edges. When I swing, I try to turn from my center. I don't want to just sway back, I want to turn from the center engaging my big muscles as I coil from a solid balanced base transferring the energy and unloading on my golf ball.

This mantra is just as important to my partners and me in our business. We believe we need to operate from a strong base, which could be interpreted as living by our personal core values, operating our firm based on our values and mission, building the skill sets that will be instrumental to our success, or staying true to ourselves to find happiness.

For many of us, having balance in our lives is essential to maintaining our sanity. Anytime our lives get too narrowly focused for too long, that lopsidedness starts to take its toll on our mental and physical health ... as well as our families. I am a classic case. I am a workaholic. If it wasn't for Michaelle, I would be so addicted to work that I probably wouldn't take time to bathe. I certainly wouldn't stay in shape, take the time I do now to play golf, to ski, to spend time relaxing with the family. It is easy for me to get out of balance, out of shape, and living an unhealthy, dissatisfying life by chasing the next accomplish-ment and looking for that next "high" I get from achievement. Overachievers commonly fall into this trap. The problem is, while achievement might drive me, it does not fulfill me or sustain my happi-ness. So, like an alcoholic avoiding the next taste of wine, I am sharing with you that balance is critical to my sanity and openly admitting that it is easy for me lose my way without constant vigilance.

The final element is "having a target or direction in mind." Engage with your life. Whatever it is you want to do, stop making excuses and go for it. Figure out what you want to achieve, prioritize those desires, and start working smarter about the level of resources you devote to each effort rather than constantly mismanaging those resources and having to work harder to make up for it. As you think about wherever you are, or whatever step you are taking within your plan, ask yourself to identify the base you are operating from and how can you go about improving it. As you consider maintaining your balance, characterize what that means to you and what signs you need to look for to indicate that you might be starting to shift to an imbalanced situation. As you reflect on your target, ensure that you are actively engaged and doing an appropriate (not excessive) amount of work to achieve the objective of your choice.

If you recall the computer cable company I mentioned in chapter 2, "Desire," their base was their market share and reputation for making cables. They became out of balance when too much of their executive focus and strategy was misplaced leveraging a short-term non-core computer memory market. Their focus was diffused with multiple strategies, which led them into trouble. The fact is, I am commonly brought into situations today where companies have lost sight of the necessary synergy that needs to be maintained with base, center, and intent. The value is in keeping all three top of mind.

From a personal perspective, I have a tendency to get out of balance if I am not constantly vigilant. Being a frequent flier with over three mil-lion total miles under my belt, I know the flight attendant security-briefing all too well. One of the statements they cover is about protocol when the oxygen masks drop from the ceiling. They say "put your oxygen mask on first before assisting others." Why would they say this, especially if you were sitting beside your own child? Wouldn't you want to put an oxygen mask on your child first? The answer is no! You put your mask on first so that you have the clarity of thought to assist your child or those around you. If you put the oxygen mask on your child or someone else needing assistance first, you may quickly pass out and not be available to help anyone. Because others, like your child, will need assistance, it is important that you put yourself in a position to provide it. Fortunately, my wife is really good about putting her oxygen mask on (making sure her life is in balance) so that she is well positioned to come in and save me from myself. The school's martial arts mantra of building on a strong base, maintaining balance, and engaging (intent and focus) with what is important is a great daily reminder for me to keep focused on the basics so that I am not only working better, but getting better from the foundation up.

Assess yourself on keeping foundation top of mind throughout everything you do. Circle how you feel you are doing. On this subject, I:

Need a lot of work	Need a little work	Am okay	Feel good where I am

Take a few minutes and consider the following so that you can work better rather than more:

What do you consider to be your base?

_____

_____

_____

How would you define being "in-balance" for yourself?

_____

_____

_____

Where is your intent (what are your trying to achieve and do you have a clear target in mind)?

_____

_____

_____

(continued)

What can you do to improve your overall foundation, syncing base, balance and intent?

_____

_____

_____

Investing in Loss

"Invest in loss" is a technique that helps us expand our knowledge and ability by setting our ego aside so that we can learn how to work better and get better. With invest-in-loss, the focus is on improving; whether you win or lose, whether you look bad or like a pro, whether you are embarrassed or held up as an example, the key is to improve. Don't confuse investing in loss with "give up and don't care." These two phrases have nothing in common. While investing in loss still means you are trying, you are not restricting yourself to those approaches that give you the best chance of "winning."

To be fair, I regularly struggle with this technique. I don't struggle with the message, because it fits in with my belief of embracing failure, but I do struggle with its implementation. Because there is a competitive aspect to martial arts, the issue is accentuated in this environment. For instance, as a black belt, if I am teaching a lower level belt a specific technique, shouldn't I be able to do it better than he or she does? If I am engaged in a sparring match with that same person, shouldn't I win the engagement if I am going to demonstrate that I am worthy of wearing my higher ranking of black belt? The answer, though it might feel like it should be "yes," is "no." If I am always trying to "win," that mindset will require me to limit myself to using only my strengths while rarely developing my weaknesses. If this is my approach, when my skills plateau or start to dwindle, which they will, then the only example I will be setting is that I am not worthy of wearing my black belt.

There is another aspect to this. It is about obtaining a more honest and accurate self-report as to where you are. For example, let's say I am being taught how to throw someone. There are steps to follow, like what body part to grab, how to grab it, integrating your body with theirs at the right place for the throw, using your body to create leverage, making sure the person being thrown is kept safe, and so forth. However, if I am much bigger than the person I am about to throw, unless my focus is on investing in loss, I could easily call on my physical strength to execute the technique and mask the fact that I was improperly performing it. The problem is ... on the day that I would be required to throw someone my size or larger, I wouldn't have the requisite skills because I never learned the proper techniques in the first place. So, for me to learn how to throw someone well, I need to let the techniques I am trying to develop stand on their own in order to determine how well they are working. Or, put another way, I need to try those new techniques with the mindset that if failure seems imminent, I will invest in loss, keep my ego in check, and I will stay focused on executing the technique whether or not it works.

Now, think about this book. I have techniques throughout it for you to consider. When you decide a technique is worth attempting, do it with an "invest in loss" attitude. Don't modify the technique to something that you are already comfortable doing because you think it has a better chance of success. Work the technique; then let the wisdom from the work bubble up so that you can see how to leverage it to be of the greatest benefit to you. Learning to work better often starts with the invest-in-loss attitude.

Assess yourself at investing in loss. Circle how you feel you are doing. On this subject, I:

Need a lot of work	Need a little work	Am okay	Feel good where I am

How are you investing in loss to uncover your real weaknesses so that you can take action now, to either strengthen them or mitigate their negative impact, before you rely on them to the point that they hurt you? Where can I apply the invest in loss technique to help me work better?

_____

_____

_____

Third "Bad" and You're Out

This is a philosophy that I adopted years ago while I was reflecting on a number of situations that had gone wrong as I was doing the work. As I have mentioned numerous times before, when we make mistakes (and for me that is often), that tends to trigger a time of great reflection. One day, I noticed a trend. As I would reflect on events ending negatively, I realized that in almost every case, my mistakes had compounded before they hurt me. So, for this discussion, when I refer to a "bad," this is simply a short hand way of saying "I made a mistake."

A simple example of one of my bads was a ticket I received for speeding. I hate getting tickets because it seems unfair given that I mostly drive like the proverbial little old lady—slowly. When I thought about how I got my ticket, I realized that my driving faster than the speed limit was not my first mistake. That was just when I got caught. My first mistake was trying to squeeze more activities into my available time than could be realistically accomplished. So, I allowed my poor time management to put me 20 minutes late for my scheduled departure to the airport to catch my plane. Because of this, the entire time I was driving, I was feeling a great deal of anxiety worrying about whether I would miss my flight. During that 25 mile drive, I ran multiple yellow lights and one very, very orange one. Finally, I got pulled over for speeding. In this scenario, I made numerous mistakes, but I got caught only for the last one. Even at that, I was very fortunate because I had set myself up for consequences far worse.

For example, I could have missed my flight and had I not been able to get to my client's retreat on time, I would have, at a minimum, disappointed them or could have been fired altogether. What's worse, by being cavalier about managing my anxiety, I could have pushed myself to have an aneurysm or a heart attack, something my dad had several of before he died. Finally, by running the red light—okay I called it orange earlier—I could have hit someone and hurt them or myself, thereby impacting the rest of my life (either mental or physical jail for carelessly hurting someone, including myself). All of this was made possible because of my first bad. My response should have been, "I mismanaged my time. While I will drive faster than my normal pokiness, I will not speed or run lights. I will accept the consequences of my first mistake without compounding them into something that is probably far worse." Even with all of this, I still made my flight. I walked on, about $150 poorer and very frustrated, literally just as they shut the aircraft door. But the fact is I was frustrated about the wrong thing. I was focusing on the delay caused because I got a ticket rather than the rash of bad judgments I had made along the way.

Another example that comes to mind pertains to a trip I took several years ago from Breckenridge to work with a client in Florida. I was in Breckenridge on vacation with my family, but I was going to leave for a few days to facilitate an executive meeting with a client. In order to get to Florida from Breckenridge, I had to catch a 5:30 am shuttle to get to the Denver airport so that I could arrive at my destination in time to have dinner with my client. Thus far, I was "bad" free. After arriving, that evening, dehydrated by the travel, I had a few drinks during the dinner festivities: my first bad. Then, even though I knew I had to be ready for an 8:30 am meeting, I stayed out a little later than I should have with the client. Now don't jump to conclusions. I am old, so late for me was about 10:00 pm. But still, given the role the facilitator plays in a retreat and the need for me to be mentally sharp, this was my second bad. Because I like to decompress before I can go to sleep, I watched TV for about an hour and a half to stop my mind from spinning about the conversations at dinner and the meeting I was going to facilitate the next morning. This left me with the possibility of a maximum of six-and-a-half hours of sleep: my third bad. After an all-day meeting, the group goes to dinner to relax and reflect on the high points of the day. Once again, I don't get a normal eight hours of sleep, which would be okay except for the fact that I was already operating with a sleep deficit: my fourth bad. Because I was tired, to stay awake and sharp during the next day, I drank several extra caffeinated drinks and not nearly enough water: my fifth bad. After the second day, I hopped on a plane and flew back to Denver. I then caught a shuttle into the mountains. By the time I arrived back at the house in Breckenridge (it was at 10,000 feet), I was very tired, dehydrated, and what a surprise ... I got altitude sickness. I know from experience to avoid going into the mountains exhausted or dehydrated, and the rule is that you *never* go in both exhausted and dehydrated. That is a guaranteed formula for a terrible experience. The fact is that I got altitude sickness because I allowed five bad decisions to compound. With any one or two of them, I most likely would have been fine. After reflection regarding a number of previous situations, along with tracking this phenomenon once I became aware of it, while you might get caught sooner, in my experience, you can count on getting caught by the third compounded bad choice in a row. If you get away with more choices, then you are just lucky.

What my analysis taught me is that a single small mistake often doesn't hurt you ... but you can be assured that compounding one mistake on another will. When you find things going wrong as you try to achieve your objectives, look for a series of compounded bad decisions. Then, make sure you don't add another mistake on top of what is already in play. This acceptance of the first mistake and your willingness to face the fallout for it will help you avoid the more costly "three bads and you're out" consequences.

Assess yourself on being aware of compounding "bads." Circle how you feel you are doing. On this subject, I:

Need a lot of work	Need a little work	Am okay	Feel good where I am

How can I keep this concept in mind so that I can catch myself compounding "bads" before they hurt me? In what areas or situations do I tend to commonly compounds "bads?"

Stay in the Present

Have you ever caught yourself daydreaming and realized a significant amount of time has passed while you were on autopilot and you can't remember any details in-between? In the beginning, when I was driving back and forth between Austin and Arlington when Michaelle was earning her Ph.D., I found that there were times when my mind would get immersed in a topic and when I came back to the present, I might have driven between 50 and 100 miles. I couldn't remember passing through cities. I did make the drive often, so the road was familiar, but what a scary thought that I was driving a death machine at 70 miles an hour on a crowded freeway and had no recollection of my navigation for such a long distance.

It is hard to stay in the present. Our minds like to drift. As a matter of fact, I don't believe we can stop them from starting to drift. But I do know we can stop them from *continuing* to drift. We start thinking about what could be, or what is, or what went wrong and before you know it, we are like sleep walkers only partially aware. You would think this mental wandering would occur only in a relaxed festive environment (like floating in the water with a cold beer in your hands), but I can find myself drifting playing sports, engaged in a conversation, in the heat of a conflict, or doing almost anything. While I usually won't migrate for long in very active circumstances, I certainly might drift for seconds or even a minute or two. Staying in the present means that all of your attention, not just part of it, is tuned-in to right now.

By staying in the now as much as possible, you will reap many benefits. Consider minor benefits like remembering someone's name after an introduction. Why do we forget so often? Because most of us aren't in the now. We are thinking about what we are going to say, or admiring the way that person is dressed, or considering any number of ideas. We don't remember that person's name because, technically, our mind was not present at the time of the introduction.

Where I see people experience immediate negative results for separating from the moment is when they get mad at themselves for something they just did. I struggle with this. The rational part of my brain can be quickly overwhelmed by the emotional part of it. But for every second my head is wrapped around my current failure, I stand a greater chance of compounding that with another failure because I am no longer operating in the now. In golf, I try to let the bad shot go and focus only on what I am doing right now with my next one. In martial arts, I have to forget that I just poorly executed a big-air break fall and get my head back into the present or I will likely really hurt myself with my next attempt. As a facilitator (consultant), I have to stay in the present all meeting long because I know that anytime I slip away, I not only have an excellent chance of missing important information, but that wandering might prohibit me from being able to find a solution for my client.

Tune into your life as it is happening right now and you will find joy and pleasure all around you. By the way, if you decide to use "now" to do something special for yourself—like relax, play a sport, read—don't diminish that experience by beating yourself up the whole time because you feel like you should be actively pursuing some item on your to-do list. The more and the longer you can stay in the present, the easier it will be for you to find ways to work better, work smarter, and avoid defaulting to working longer and harder.

Assess yourself on staying in the present throughout the day. Circle how you feel you are doing. On this subject, I:

Need a lot of work	Need a little work	Am okay	Feel good where I am

List a few situations where you know you are having a hard time staying in the present? What signals can you monitor that will alert you that you are starting to drift?

_____

_____

_____

Get Better, Work Better, Right Now

Whatever you decide you want to improve or accomplish takes effort. Relationships take effort. Your job takes effort. Having fun takes effort. Know that whatever is important to you could easily start to wither away if you don't give it the right amount of attention.

Imagine that you are growing tomatoes. On a very regular and consistent basis, if you want ripe juicy tomatoes to eat, they need care (a little water, a little sun, a little nourishment, protection from insects or birds). Too much or too little water and they are dead. Too much or too little sun and they are dead. Too much or too little protection and they are ruined. If you want homegrown tomatoes, you have to be diligent about giving them the amount of care that is needed.

Whatever you are trying to achieve in your life requires the same dynamic as growing tomatoes. In martial arts training, when you come in to work out at the school, you need to be there in mind, body, and spirit. We are not there for an aerobic workout; we are there to get better right then. Just as with growing tomatoes, it is about putting the right amount of effort into your daily regimen. If you want to come in and train for two weeks giving each workout a marginal effort and then train at your maximum once every couple of weeks—that is an example of working worse not better. As overachievers, this is a critical area for us to monitor; putting in the time but not focusing the effort. That kind of approach is similar to under watering your tomatoes for 13 days and then flooding them on the 14th. Good things don't come from this type of approach for either the tomatoes or for humans. So, we have to be accountable to ourselves and think, "It is up to me to take responsibility to always try to find ways to work better, to get better, right now. I need to be vigilant about adding the right amount of effort, not too little (as I won't be pushing myself), but not too much (because I will hurt myself), so that I can sustain this focus over a long period of time."

Included in this same theme is the idea that we have to "be included in our own calendars." Recently, coaching an overachiever friend, we had a discussion about things she wanted to do to improve her life. During those discussions, she talked about fulfilling her obligations at work, meeting the expectations of her kids, taking care of her aging mother and father, spending time with her husband and so on. As she finished her story, she said, "As soon as I get all of that taken care of, I can focus on what is important to me." The problem is ... that time will never come! I am not suggesting that you don't have obligations to others. But I am emphatically reminding you that you also have an obligation to yourself. You need to treat "taking care of yourself" and "fulfilling your desires" as to-do items on your own life-calendar and understand that they deserve some of your attention on a regular basis.

One more thought occurs to me as I discuss this topic. It is based on a phrase in John's schools philosophy. As you do the work, be firm enough with yourself that you stay focused and push yourself to the edge every day to get better. But also be gentle enough that you realize that we are not always at our best, our lives are complicated, and giving it your best effort every day is not the same as being the best you can be every day. So be gentle enough with yourself that you can get better and working better even when you are operating at a sub-par performance level.

Assess yourself on whether you are trying to work better and get better right now. Circle how you feel you are doing. On this subject, I:

Need a lot of work	Need a little work	Am okay	Feel good where I am

What are you doing to find ways to work better, get better right now? Where in your life are you misallocating your resources; either overwatering or under watering something that is important to you?

_____

_____

_____

Path Wrap-Up

Doing the Work is rarely a problem for the overachiever, but sustaining the right level of effort and learning to work better often is. Overachievers often over-water one objective while under-watering several others that are of equal importance to them. Therefore, for those who are looking for ways to overachieve on multiple levels and on multiple objectives, I have introduced techniques in this chapter to help you be more efficient and effective in your efforts to continue the work and to work better.

See the expanded flowchart below that includes the Work step covered in this chapter. The graphics that include the letters A, B, or C are page connectors. Page connector A takes us to the second page of the flowchart (which I will unveil as soon as I have introduced that material). And page connectors B and C are the return points from the second page to this page of the flowchart. So here is a look at the Process which includes both **Desire** and the **Work**:

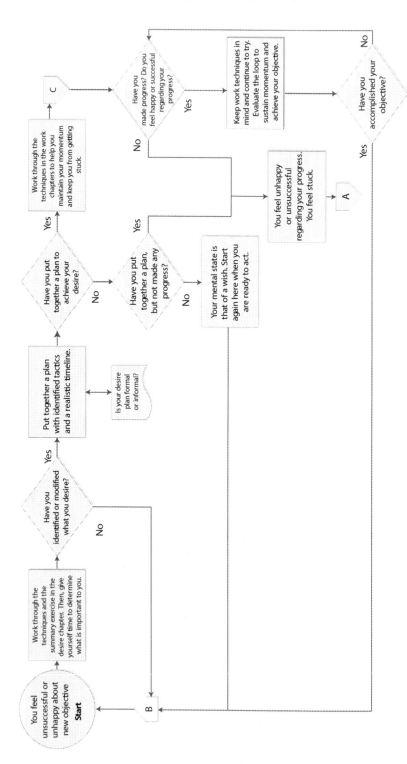

Chapter 4
Overarching Concepts That Apply to Getting Unstuck

As you can see from the flowchart at the end of chapter 3, if you have identified a desire, created a plan and are working your plan to your satisfaction, you are in what I refer to as the "Try (Work)-Evaluate" loop which continues until you accomplish whatever you want to achieve. As long as you recognize the early warning signals and respond to them in a timely way, you will remain unstuck, continuing to work better and achieve more.

However, most of us are not that fortunate. We start getting stuck and rather than respond to the early warning signals, we either ignore them, hoping they will go away or try to power through them. Unfortunately, my experience is that neither of these approaches works well very often. Therefore, we get kicked out of the Try (Work)-Evaluate loop due to our dissatisfaction (our feelings of being unsuccessful or unhappy about our progress or priorities). This chapter introduces new concepts and expands on a couple mentioned in previous chapters that permeate every aspect of this Process, from determining your desire, doing the work, recognizing the early warning signals, to following the paths to getting unstuck ("What You *Are* Thinking" and "What You *Are* Doing").

The first concept, "Let It Go," was included in the introduction. But in that context, I was asking you to let go of what you think you know as a precursor to reading the rest of the book. However, at this point, I am covering why this foundational concept is so important to the successful implementation of my Process as well as how to use it.

Let It Go

"Let It Go" is a trigger phrase John uses to let his students know he sees them resisting change, holding on too tightly to the past, beating themselves up for a prior mistake, allowing their egos to cloud their judgment and so on. The meaning behind "Let it Go" is as simple as the phrase itself: Don't let your thoughts, expectations, tension, personal baggage, vanity, ego—you name it—get in your way of getting better. John will often pose the question to me, and everyone else at the school for that matter, "What do you need to let go of right now to allow yourself to get better right now?" As well, in our conversations about various struggles I might be facing, the same question is posed, "What do you need to let go of so that you can get unstuck and moving again?" I can tell you from personal experience—what you need to let go of could be anything. But ultimately it will come down to letting go of something you think you already know. We typically don't act until we believe we understand or know something. It may be as simple as defensiveness because you don't want to be proven wrong (because I *know* the importance of being "right") or don't want to acknowledge that you have made a mistake because I *know* that mistakes are synonymous with being a failure). It could be that you are frustrated by your progress which is being held back because you are more focused on winning than learning (because I *know* that winning is really more important than learning). While there are plenty of examples throughout the book, the point is ... anytime you are starting to get stuck or are stuck, chances are that you need to let go of something which will likely be rooted in what you think you know.

Letting go is difficult to do because it requires an honest self-report as to what is in your way. Given that what you are reading now is the fourth rewrite of this material, with several additional reorganizations as well, imagine the conversation I had with John when he suggested that this version was necessary. I was very frustrated, and very irritated ... with him. Why would I be mad at him? He was only trying to make the book better. I just didn't want to hear it. I knew my previous version was just fine. I knew that the next version wouldn't be much different—it would just prolong the time required to get the book published. That night, I remember clearly the conversation (in my head) that allowed me to transition so I could get started on the fourth rewrite. I had to let go of the idea that the current version of this book was a clear presentation of the ideas. I asked myself "What is more important ... to get this project done according to the plan and timeline

I had laid out, or make the book better?" It wasn't a hard decision to make once I opened myself to learning more and trusting that John's assessment that we were not where we needed to be was enough to justify the delay. To be clear, I was wrong in what I thought I knew, because based on what I know now, the extra time helped resolved some holes that I didn't want to admit were in the previous versions. But notice the trap. What I thought I knew created resistance to writing version four of the book, but what I know now regarding version four could create resistance regarding what I am able to learn in the future. So, we have to constantly let go of what we think we know in order to better position ourselves for what we are about to learn.

What also makes this concept difficult to implement at times is that what we need to let go of could be some aspect or the priority of one of our personal core values. Sometimes when we get stuck, the only way to get unstuck is to rethink about the various values we have that we have never bothered to challenge because we consider them unchangeable components of who we are. We often blindly accept those values and their priority as being valid in perpetuity. In martial arts, I see this conflict between core values and learning arising frequently. While students, including me, are practicing various techniques on our own, this isn't much of an issue. But as soon as a particular exercise creates a physical engagement between two or three people, well, that is a different story. All of a sudden, the fear of losing, or the fear of getting hurt, or the ego to look good, or most likely, the desire to win, takes over and the learning process comes to a halt. We lose sight of what the exercise was trying to teach us in the first place: creating a controlled situation where the intensity is amped up to see how well everyone manages their minds, controls their emotions, and stays in the now. In order to get better, faster, and stronger in martial arts, you commonly are asked to let go of, or better put, reprioritize those beliefs that no longer serve you. In this case, while a competitive spirit is great, a competitive attitude that is always at the highest priority is not only out of balance, but can be very damaging. You have to know when and how to reduce its priority or you will find yourself stuck often. This is a predominant reason so many people end up quitting before completing their objectives; they were unwilling to let go of the priority of a core value in order to allow them to think differently. Or put another way, they are unwilling to let go of what they think they know about the priority of a specific idea, value, or belief.

To further clarify reprioritization in the context of letting go, here is another example. Consider that someone has a very high priority for being honest and trustworthy in their dealings with others. But also consider that this same person has a high priority, although a lower one, for meeting a specific financial goal. Now let's picture a scenario where this person has an opportunity to make a big sale and all that is required to close the deal is to forget to bring up some important information to the buyer. In this case, in order to make the sale, this person would have to compromise the higher priority, honesty, for a lower priority, achieving the financial goal. Because this person's values would be in conflict in this scenario, even if he or she decided to make the sale and got away with it, this act would likely create emotional chaos as he or she tried to resolve it internally. Though as humans we are good at finding ways to ease this kind of pain through rationalizations like "buyer beware," or "it's not personal, it's business," if the conflict exists, your mind will still require you to reconcile the disconnect. Or in some cases, when what you are thinking is in direct conflict with what you want to do, that conflict won't allow you to take action at all. Now, if honesty is not important to you, (and that is your choice; I am simply creating an emotional scenario to make a point) then this example is meaningless, because not being forthcoming would not have violated a core belief. So in order to keep from getting stuck, the general rule is

> *If you have to comprise your values or beliefs in order reach some objective ... or compromise a higher priority value or belief to achieve a lower one, then either (1) change your objective (change your desire, plan, tactics), or (2) change or redefine the priority of your values or beliefs in relation to each other.*

Don't be surprised as you challenge the priority of some of your ideas, core beliefs or values against others that you find it is time to update them due to changes in your thinking. For instance, a common one for overachievers might be that you believe "You need to be hard on yourself if you want to improve your performance." While ideas such as this one might have played a positive role in your past, that doesn't mean that it is working for you now, or that you should continue to hold on to it or that you should maintain it with its same priority.

Being able to "Let Go of What You Think You Know" is the cornerstone of this process, regardless of what you are doing, what you are thinking, or where you are in the cycle. What bias, belief, process, vanity, insecurity, fear, expectation, outcome, permission, acceptance, and the like do you need to let go of or embrace to allow you to change what you think. "What do I need to let go of right now?" is truly the billion dollar question you will find yourself asking and answering every day, and every moment, you find yourself stuck or tarting to get stuck. By letting go of something, you can get back on the road to feeling happy or successful about whatever it is you are trying to achieve.

This leads me to the next concept that applies to every aspect of the Process—Become the lead programmer.

Become the Lead Programmer

Your mind is the most powerful resource available to you. It is easy to think of it as a super-computer, running your physical being; constantly compiling data, processing complex transactions, creating internally revealed reports, and so on. We know through research that most of us barely tap into our brain's full capability, so it is also not hard to get complacent and deem the brain to be some magical organ that we just hope keeps running properly. As well, it is easy for us to get comfortable interacting with our minds as if we were only data entry operators rather than the brain's lead programmer.

With this perspective in mind, doesn't it make sense that a key focus to finding the success and happiness you desire is to learn to better manage this onboard super-computer? Most people try to manage it through influence; changing our way of thinking by constantly having the mind process new data. This approach usually takes a lot of time because dramatic change requires an overwhelming amount of new data to modify or refute positions and beliefs with which we have grown comfortable. We have all heard the historically used tag-line of the NAACP in its initiatives and advertisements: "A mind is a terrible thing to waste." Because of the minimal effort many people make to challenge and control this incredible asset, we've become comfortable wasting it. So, while the "new data" approach can be effective over time, I believe there are more powerful, more direct, and quicker ways to change our minds through "reprogramming."

Consider tension, fear, worry, guilt, duty, failure, permission, and more. Most of the time, these reactions or emotions are not about reality, but rather, our mind's current interpretations. These interpretations instantly cause intellectual, psychological, and physiological responses. So, how do we reprogram our minds to work more to our advantage? There are a number of strategies to consider.

The first is to calm it. Meditation is known to be a fantastic tool that can rein in the chaos which often overwhelms us. Meditation doesn't have to last hours to be valuable ... you can focus your mind, clear out the frantic thoughts and change the way you feel in seconds. For example, consider that for most of my life, I had high blood pressure readings every time I went to see my doctor. The fact is ... I don't normally have high blood pressure (I know this because I frequently monitor my blood pressure at home with a machine that is regularly benchmarked against those in my doctor's office). But for years, all I would have to do was be in one of those doctor's stalls and my blood pressure would shoot up 20 points (both diastolic and systolic), along with my heart rate. After I learned how to calm my mind, "the white coat syndrome" physiological responses vanished.

Meditation is about focus. The easiest way to do this is to fix your mind on one point or one thought. Just listening to your breathing is the simplest idea. To augment that, as thoughts come into your mind, don't analyze them, don't process them, don't respond to them, just observe them and let them fly right back out. Don't hold on to them! When you focus entirely on your breathing, you will find in seconds that your mind clears, emotions fade, pain may subside, and so much more. By incorporating this seconds-to-minutes meditative approach into your life, you can have an instant impact on the way you think, which will give you better control over your actions, responses, and emotions.

While meditation can instantly reprogram the mind, there are other approaches as well. I mentioned the most common one above; reprogramming through learning. Another way to reprogram the mind is by trying to observe a situation from a different perspective. As we expand our perspective and awareness, we can easily change our beliefs or world views. Here is an experience that comes to mind:

> My stepdaughter, Cheri, and I had numerous conflicts in her late teenage years and early twenties. Fortunately for me, we both outgrew them and have a wonderful relationship today. However, one of our confrontations had deteriorated to the point that Michaelle decided it would be beneficial to get help. We knew Karl Krumm Ph.D., a friend of ours and psychologist could provide that assistance. The conflict was over who paid for college. My rule, and yes, I unfortunately had a lot of rules back then, was that as long as Cheri brought home B's or above, we would pay for everything (books, tuition, living expenses). Cheri thought I was being too controlling and was frustrated by the unnecessary pressure I was adding to her life. I thought she was being too spoiled and was frustrated by her feelings of entitlement. We were at an impasse. I clearly remember sitting with Cheri, Michaelle, and Karl as I laid out my view of the situation. Karl then asked Cheri to do the same. He also asked her if earning "Bs" was difficult for her to which she replied that it was not but that my approach was just adding unnecessary pressure.

> I can still remember the comments Karl made immediately after we were both done defending our positions. First, he looked at me with his brows furrowed and said, "You need to lighten up." Then, he looked at Cheri and said, "You might be looking at this all wrong. What you are hearing is that if you don't perform up to his standards, he will punish you and take away something you want. What he is also saying, that I believe you are overlooking, is that as long as you make "or better, he *can't* take his support away. Have you thought about how much control you have over this situation, especially given the lack of difficulty you have in maintaining the grade-point average

required? You are in control ... he isn't! While Bill set up the
terms of the agreement, he also has to live with them."

Well, needless to say, Cheri was much happier after that counseling
session—much happier than I was at first. While I had not thought of
our situation the way Karl described it, he was right; I had to abide by
the agreement. Both of us adopted a new perspective immediately,
including the need for me to lighten up. As Cheri and I expanded our
perspectives of the situation, our views and beliefs changed. When
Cheri came to the meeting, she was mad because she felt she had no
control. By the time she left, she realized she had a great deal of
control, not only of her life, but over her college funding as well. In
reality, however, nothing had actually changed except our perspectives!
By the way, while Cheri and I were fighting over this issue, she had
never brought home grades less than a B anyway. This was simply a
conflict over a principle. Here was a case where it was easy to
reprogram the mind by viewing the situation from another angle.

The overall message here is that we need to take on the lead
programmer role when it comes to constantly reprograming our minds
and stop defaulting to being just data entry operators. We can change
our beliefs, values, emotions, thoughts, physical responses, and
psychological responses in mere seconds. This dynamic resource
prompted one of the fundamental concepts of this book, which is

All you have to do to be different is to think differently!

Wow ... can it really be this simple? I certainly believe it is. John and I
see transformations every day in training and coaching as people leap
from one skill level to the next simply because they let something go
which allowed them to start thinking differently. Or, they have been
able to instantly lighten the load they have been carrying just by challenging why they are thinking the way they do.

The Actions That Letting Go Unveils to Help You Get Unstuck

While I introduced these actions at the beginning of the book, it is time
to get a little better understanding of how to leverage them. At any
point in time, when you realize you are dissatisfied with your level of
success or happiness, once you have decided what to let go of that was
the source of the negative emotions you are feeling, you will end up
making at least one—if not two or all three—of these choices. You can

1. modify your Desire or redefine your plan-tactics, timeframe or
   expectations. I call this action "replan"; or

2. prioritize what is important to you (which often includes reconsidering the priority of deep seeded beliefs or values). I call this action "reprioritize"; or

3. maintain your Desire but break the emotional link between your Desire and your progress or priorities. I call this action "reaffirm."

To help you better conceptualize the choices you have to help you regain your momentum, I have put together a simple dissatisfaction scenario for your review:

Desire and expectations: By the time I earn my black belt, I will be able to easily execute all of my kicks to at least solar plexus height, with many at face height. My plan is to work out two to three times a week for the seven to eight years it will take for me to earn my black belt, which should be plenty of time to build the requisite flexibility and abilities

Work (Try): For more than 20 years, I have been practicing martial arts. While I have to manage my work out schedule around my business commitments (which takes me out of town a great deal), when I am at home, I typically work out three to four, and sometimes five days a week

Evaluate: At a recent instructor's clinic, I realized that I had the lowest kicks of any black belt during that training session. From that clear perspective and comparison, I realized that I was unhappy about my level of progress pertaining to my flexibility and the height of my kicks

Once I recognized my level of frustration, the Process would have sent me to work through "What You *Are* Thinking" (chapter 5) and "What You *Are* Doing" (chapter 6). As I read through that material, here is a thought that one of the techniques in these chapters could have easily invoked:

New Thoughts: I realized that my level of dissatisfaction began right after the demonstration as I evaluated my performance against those around me. As I was rereading the techniques, I was reminded that martial arts is about self-improvement, not about ego. I recalled that I have never been as flexible as others and this has always been my slowest area of improvement. I considered the work I have been doing to make incremental improvement given the limited range of motion in my ankles and hip flexors. As I thought through all of this, I recognized how much progress I have made regarding my flexibility overall and even as recently as in the last few months.

With this new thinking, I have several actions I can take mentally that will likely dissolve my level of dissatisfaction and allow me to go back to work improving my flexibility and kicking skills. These actions include replanning, reprioritizing, or reaffirming my desire. Here is an example of each of these applied to this scenario.

> **Replan**: In this case, I have decided that my desire of kicking at the minimum height of the solar plexus with many at face height, given my limitation of flexibility was too grandiose. Therefore, my fine-tuned desire is that each year for the next five years my kicks will be higher than ever before as compared to the previous April rank exam.

The focus of my goal shifted from kicking as high as everyone else to continuing to do the work necessary to improve my flexibility. I realized that my plan, tactics, and expectations were identified long before I understood the extent of my inflexibility of my ankles and hips. Therefore, I am going to build this information into my replan and create new tactics and expectations. Going forward, I will also try to keep top of mind that I need to be comparing my current performance against my past performance and not to the performance of others. After letting go of the ego that drove my dissatisfaction, I realized that while I could not perform in this area as well as the average black belt, overall I was satisfied that I was still making progress. This redefinition of my kicking desire not only would allow my lack-of-success feelings to disappear, but restart my momentum to put in the effort necessary to improve the height of my kicks over the next five years.

> **Reprioritize**: In this variation, I have decided that my desire of kicking at the minimum height of the solar plexus with many at face height is reasonable for me to expect. However, recognizing that flexibility will likely always be an area requiring extra work, I remind myself that kicking is just one tool in the martial arts self-defense toolkit. As I considered this, I decided that while the height of my kicks was still important, they should have a far lower priority than the number and overall quality of tools that I was building in my toolkit.

As I reflected on the multitude of techniques I have developed over the years that are part of my martial arts toolkit, I realized that I was satisfied with where I was, happy with the direction I was going and feeling good about my progress. Reprioritizing in this scenario wouldn't make me feel good about the level of my kicks, but it would likely resolve my dissatisfaction since it would compel me to compare that single aspect of my performance against the progress I have been making regarding the broader skill set I was developing.

> **Reaffirm**: I have always had a great deal of respect for people that can kick high. High kicks are predominant in any martial arts movie and they are certainly what martial artists like to show in demonstrations. Given this and my long-term commitment to martial arts, I am going to maintain the goal of being able to execute very high kicks.

You can have great martial arts skills, but many of them are indiscernible to the untrained eye (like control over your breathing, tension, mind, and such). But high kicks are a very visible and outward sign of skill. Therefore, I am going to hold on to my desire. However, unlike the two examples above, I am not creating a new plan with lower expectations because I still want to believe that any day now I will be able to kick per my original plan. Also, I am not going to reprioritize the importance of high kicks against some other desire I have because I want my kicking to remain a high priority for me. By choosing the reaffirmation action, I am deciding to disconnect the emotional link between my high kicking priority and my progress. I will work on it each day, with an expectation to be able to execute my kicks exactly as I imagine, but if I don't, I will simply evaluate that shortfall without emotion and just keep working to improve. As many of you would guess, this is probably the hardest action for most overachievers to take.

I think one of the reasons overachievers perform so high consistently is that we tend to internalize and attach a lot of emotion to objectives we take on. We commit ourselves to it, which is great. But that level of commitment also commonly allows our performance to define us. Our commitment and focus is one of our great strengths, but it can become our weakness as well. For me, there are numerous aspects of my life where I have a very high emotional connection to my performance. For instance, when I play golf and score poorly, that bothers me. Conversely, Michaelle can go out and play a round of golf and if her performance is not up to expectation, it doesn't really bother her as she will likely say something like "I had a great time with my friends and I hit some good shots too." On the other hand, I can work with clients and give both good and bad advice and I am not nearly as critical or judgmental about that. I think that is because I absolutely know that I don't have all of the answers and as long as I am trying to do the best that I can, that is all I can ask of myself. So regarding my business, an aspect of my life that I am very proud of and is extremely important to me, I typically can emotionally detach from the results, which in my opinion helps me provide better advice. Yet I struggle breaking that same link in other areas of my life.

Changing the Way You Think

The realization that all we have to do to be different is to allow ourselves to think differently is very powerful. The great news is ... it's often not that hard, and sometimes it is downright easy, once you focus your attention on the right places.

Before I went through the cathartic steps of working with John to come up with this Process and refining my thoughts on this topic, I would occasionally go through some multi-day bouts with gloom. I don't want to say that I would get depressed because that would be too harsh of a descriptor. Something would happen, such as I would find out that a potential client did not select our firm for an engagement, or a conflict within my extended family would take center stage, a health issue would arise, or some other negative encounter would come to my attention. If I was already in a highly stressed state, when this news would hit, my outlook could instantly shift from positive to a state of melancholy. I would start to worry about what might be next. None of the actual occurrences would be significant enough to alter my life, but that did not stop me from summoning up a great deal of anxiety or a sense of possible loss. For the longest time, when these kinds of sensations came over me, I just assumed it was an emotional state I had to experience and suffer through until it was over, like a cold. I never realized I could stop those negative emotions in their tracks. I was voluntarily holding onto those thoughts and trying to beat them back. My Process allows me to more quickly recognize what is happening and often let go of those thoughts with the same ease that I became aware of them.

When this doesn't work and my mind keeps churning or worrying about the data I just received, I then suggest—to myself—a different way to think. I consider the various outcomes and their likely probabilities. I accept the fact that, although unlikely, the worst case scenario might occur, with the commitment to myself that I am ready to face it with martial intent. Here I am letting go by considering the probabilities and accepting the idea that I will take action if and when this negative situation starts to unfold.

Between these two approaches, I can liberate myself 70 percent to 80 percent of the time from letting those negative thoughts fester into a mental burden. For the remaining 20 percent to 30 percent of the negative thoughts that still linger after these two approaches fail, I interface directly with the "Let It Go" concept. I immediately ask myself, "What am I holding on to that is magnifying this issue or escalating my emotions?" In a benign situation a couple of years ago, after weeks of deadlines and pressure, I experienced an insignificant event (a client decided to cancel a large project that was about to begin) that created an overwhelming negative feeling. Surprised by the intensity of my reaction, I focused on what I needed to let go of. I quickly realized after I asked this question that I was about ready to make a significant investment in equipment for our video studio that would allow us to offer some exciting new products. I knew that this financial setback would derail that project which I was more enthusiastic about than I realized. After I recognized what I was subconsciously holding onto, it was easy for me to stop locking into my plan, put off that investment and wait until our reserve cash flow returned. Within a short period of time, new opportunities replaced the disappearing one and the project was put back on the schedule. It usually is not hard to find out what you need to let go of as soon as you realize that letting go is what you are searching for.

This reminds me of a heart-warming story in a wonderful book about the resilience and redemption of the human spirit. It is a story about Louis Zamperini and his extraordinary life in the book *Unbroken* by Laura Hillenbrand. Here was a man who had survived numerous devastating experiences, including being lost at sea and suffering lengthy torture at a Japanese prisoner of war camp. Here was a man that after the Second World War lived a life full of anger and rage because of the horrors he had experienced. One night, he very reluctantly agreed to go with his wife to hear the evangelist Billy Graham preach. There was one condition that he demanded of his wife: when it came time for them to bow their heads in prayer, he wanted no part of this and they agreed they would both immediately leave. Sitting through the sermon, at various times, Louis felt "indignant rage" surging through him because of the messages he was hearing, and then it came time to pray. Louis grabbed his wife and sprinted for the exit, and in that moment he remembered a promise he made in a prayer to God on a raft in the ocean at a point when he thought he was about to die. Louis whispered, "*If you save me, I will serve you forever.*" At that single instant in time, he realized that he had survived everything and that he was not the "worthless, broken, forsaken man" he had come to believe he was. The author stated, "In a single, silent moment, his rage, his fear, his humiliation, and helplessness, had all fallen away." From this point forward, Louis's nightmares stopped and he found peace. When he thought about his past from that moment on, rather than lamenting about his suffering, he felt only the love that saved him.

For many reading this, your interpretation of this story will simply be that Louis was touched by the hand of God and born again at that moment. While I am not challenging that answer, I am going to recast the events as the author described them. Louis, who felt God had forsaken him, did not want to go hear Billy Graham. Cynthia, his wife, cajoled him into going. Louis, commonly full of rage and anger, was holding on to the experiences of his past, which kept him from moving forward. He was literally running out of the tent as the rain hitting his face reminded him of the commitment he made to God the day the rain saved his life after he drifted for weeks in a raft on the Pacific Ocean. In that instant, he realized that while he suffered terribly, he did survive. He let go of the anger and rage about the horrors of his past as he rethought his life. As of that instant, he became a different man, a happier more contented man—a man at peace with himself. I am not suggesting that God did or did not intervene here, I am simply pointing out a wonderful story about someone who experienced *a life changing thought* and lived an entirely new life from that moment forward. When you change the way you think, *you* change forever! I wanted to share this story because I thought it was such a great example, in an excellent book, about a real person, to make the point that the acceptance of an idea in your head is all it takes for you to evolve, progress, be happier, or be different.

To conclude, "Let It Go," "Become the Lead Programmer," "The Actions that Letting Go Unveils to Help You Get Unstuck" and "Changing the Way You Think" are foundational concepts that integrate with every aspect of the Process.

Chapter 5
What You *Are* Thinking

At this point in the Process, you have already identified a Desire (including a plan, tactics, timeline, and expectations) and have been following that plan doing the Work. However, for you to be at this juncture, you had to kick out of the Try (Work)-Evaluate loop because you were feeling unsuccessful or unhappy about your progress or priorities. When this negative evaluation occurs, you are either starting to get stuck or you are already stuck.

As I have observed in my experience with clients, martial arts students, and my own life, identifying a solution to get you back on track occurs by working through one of two paths. The first path is for you to consider "What You *Are* Thinking," with the second path reflecting on "What You *Are* Doing." As you consider in this chapter and the next the variety of techniques focused on what to let go of so that you can start regaining momentum, your action choices will come down to replanning, reprioritizing or reaffirming your Desire, or some combination of these. With this in mind, let's consider some techniques to help you reassess what you are thinking.

You Are Right Where You Are Supposed to Be

John often repeats the phrase "You are right where you are supposed to be" when he sees our exasperation as we try to deepen our stances or use a weapon we are unfamiliar with. A common behavior I observe among students when they realize they are struggling with something is to look around and see if they are the only ones. Misery does love company. If everyone is having a difficult time, though the frustration might continue, it is a lower level of frustration because of this contrast and compare process. However, when you are one of the few that can't get into a deeper stance or you are far clumsier than the rest regarding the use of a specific weapon, it is easy to see the aggravation pouring out. The phrase "You are right where you are supposed to be" is a reminder that the change you are looking for will come in time from the work. It highlights the idea that you have chosen to focus on other things in the past, which were important to you then and why you are who you are and where you are now. And if you focus on the work before you now, you will soon make progress here, too. This phrase is meant to take the pressure off of you so that you don't prematurely derail yourself due to ridiculous expectations.

Change comes with time. You can't do everything because your assets (time, money, resources) have a limit. Every choice you make allows you to focus on or improve one area potentially at the expense of another. While training in class, when I am beating myself up for not being a better martial artist, I have to keep in mind that had I put significantly more time into my training and become better, this reprioritization would have likely robbed me of some other skill, accomplishment, or life experience that I leverage regularly or cherish. Because we make choices every day without knowing the results those efforts will bring, we need to be willing to forgive ourselves for our errors that hindsight reveals and remember that we are right where we are supposed to be.

Assess yourself on your accepting that you are where you are supposed to be. Circle how you feel you are doing. On this subject, I:

Need a lot of work	Need a little work	Am okay	Feel good where I am

Where in my life would the concept "you are right where you are supposed to be" improve my perspective and help get me back on track towards my goal?

_____

_____

_____

Being Judgmental Is Self-Destructive

A big step in the right direction to regain momentum occurs when you start cutting yourself some slack. After you decide that you are going to make a change in your plans or objectives, it is common human behavior to beat yourself up for not arriving at that same decision earlier. On top of that, I often see people shining an intense spotlight on themselves scrutinizing every step in their progress as they start down any new path. It is almost as if we think that because we were late in making the decision, we should expect flawless performance and instant skill development to make up for the lost time. Given that progress and skill usually develop over time, putting pressure on yourself by expecting accelerated performance is a terrible idea. Not only will this pressure likely diminish the speed of your development, but I see this misguided perspective creating a level of frustration that tends to motivate people to give up rather than hang in there and get better. There is a second outcome this attitude breeds that is far less logical but unfortunately more destructive. Due to perceived lack of performance, the person subconsciously decides to hurt him or herself. This way, permission to quit is forced due to injury and no one has to admit that an obstacle couldn't be faced.

Start with the phrase "you are right where you are supposed to be." Now add, "and I accept where I am and that I am going to put together a plan to move forward at a sustainable pace." It is about making a little bit of progress every day, not a year's worth of progress in a week (because the latter, though often desired, is rarely fulfilled). Don't put yourself under your own microscope and then constantly belittle and be judgmental about every step of your performance. Being judgmental is self-destructive, not self-developing.

Assess yourself on being too judgmental or hard on yourself. Circle how you feel you are doing. On this subject, I:

Need a lot of work	Need a little work	Am okay	Feel good where I am

What am I being judgmental about that is holding me back? What should I do to stop it?

_____

_____

_____

Fear Stifles You in Every Way

Fear is an important topic to me. I believe fear is often one of the greatest offenders interfering with behavior, skill development, success, satisfaction with yourself, and happiness in your life. I am not just talking about fear as it would manifest in feelings of terror, but rather the entire range of fear, from being afraid of dying on one extreme through a simple negative thought wafting through your brain on the other.

I will start with the leftmost swing of the pendulum (the slight impact of fear) by mentioning how easy it is to hit a ball out of bounds by simply being scared you will. I remember playing golf in a tournament in high school and as I turned the front nine, I noticed that I was tied for the lead. I remember clearly taking a practice swing, standing on the 10th tee box looking down a fairly easy golf hole as I thought to myself, "whatever you do, don't go out-of- bounds to the right." Or in other words, "Bill ... don't slice your tee-shot!" I then proceeded to hit the ball a fairly long way, and while it was not clear, it looked like it barely rolled out of bounds to the right. That one negative thought—my fear of losing the lead—was all it took to create a swing malfunction so that the golf ball would go exactly where I hoped it wouldn't. As I re-teed the ball to hit a provisional shot (a second ball which I would play if the first one was found out of bounds), I thought to myself, "Don't do that again. If I do, it will be hard for me to ever make up those strokes." So I swing and hit another drive that appears to have gone on the exact same line as the previous one. Frustrated, I re-teed thinking, "If I hit this ball out of bounds, I am out of conten-tion." And again, good contact, strong hit, on the same line. Finally, and yes this story is about to come to an end, I put down my third provisional tee shot and thought to myself, "If I have to play this one, it doesn't matter." With the fear gone, I smoked the fourth ball down the middle. Hoping that one of my earlier tee shots was in-bounds, I walked up briskly to see where they finally came to rest. All three balls were lined up within two feet of each other, two feet out of bounds. I took a 12 on that hole and while I played fine the rest of the round, I wound up in the middle of the pack simply because of my outrageous score on that one hole. The fear of losing the lead was all it took to hit three of the most consistent drives in my life ... all within a small circle about 280 yards away, all out of bounds.

A very common form of fear I encounter as a consultant is fear of change, a slight pendulum move to the right. Even when we know we need to change because something in our life is not working, we invoke dysfunctional thoughts like, "I know what I am doing is not working, but what if I change and make my situation worse. I don't like being where I am, but at least it is a misery I know and a misery I can tolerate."

As the pendulum continues to swing to the right (add a little more fear), I think about how fear occasionally slips into my life at what seems to be absurd moments. I don't have to go back in time very far to think of an example. Recently, one of our standard poodles had to be put down due to kidney failure. Our other standard poodle, Delilah (Lila) who is 12 years old, was devastated by the loss of her companion. After a couple of months and a lot of crying from every member of our pack, we brought home a standard poodle puppy. Lila hated the puppy. However, she had good reason because he was kind of wild. We ended up naming him "So Ho Yen," Korean for "Tigers at Play" (based on our best interpretation of Korean), but we just call him Tiger for short. After about a month, one day out of the blue, Lila decided to interact with Tiger. Watching them just warmed our hearts. I didn't even realize how big the smile on my face was until Michaelle pointed it out. As they wrapped up whatever game they were playing and trotted back from the yard to the house together, at that moment, we knew Lila was starting to come out of her depression and that we had gotten the signal that our pack had just accepted a new member. What a high I was feeling. Now, here is the absurd part. My mind allowed me to enjoy that high for about 10 minutes, and then I starting experiencing all kinds of unprovoked negative thoughts like "I wonder how long Lila's health will hold out?"; "What happens if Tiger falls in the water and drowns and Lila loses another companion?"; and so on. Nothing actually occurred to trigger those feelings. However, my senses were flooded by this rash of paranoid thoughts that quickly wiped out my euphoria. I went from feeling great to a slight state of depression, and nothing had actually happened except for a fearful thought entering my mind!

Now, let's move the fear pendulum to the right of center to a situation in which there was and is actually a chance of being injured. I have always been a little cautious because I can still hear my dad saying to mom, "I can't take that risk because I have a family to support," when explaining why he might not ski, ride a motorcycle, and do other things that could be dangerous. Though I do take a number of risks, with his comment always running through the subconscious corridors of my mind, I find myself regularly challenging the safety reasonableness of what I am about to try. With that said, let me tell you about falling in martial arts. There are numerous ways to fall, from a soft roll, to a break fall to a wheel fall. Just as it sounds, the soft roll is fairly mild. Once you are comfortable protecting your head, neck, and back, rolling is very safe. The break fall is a little more hostile because it is learning to fall as if someone swept your feet out from under you. And finally there is the wheel fall, which embodies a movement similar to its name because your feet leave the ground following an arc shaped like a wheel (270 degrees of spin) as your legs and feet travel over your head with you landing on your side and back.

I remember the first time I was asked to execute a wheel fall with someone throwing me. I was scared, and not just a little scared. I was visualizing landing on my head and breaking-my-neck scared. And to this day, I am still slightly nervous when I execute a wheel fall for the first time after not having done one for several weeks. But here is the bad news. The most dangerous thing you can do when you need to execute a wheel fall is be reluctant. When I was first learning to fall, my fear-based instinct would influence me to fight flipping, which converted to a partial flip when thrown, resulting in painful and sometimes dangerous landings. The more times I landed badly, the more reluctant I became. I was embarrassed that I was scared, so I tried to cover it up. But John saw through that. After watching me for about 15 minutes one day, with my progress deteriorating rather than improving, he walked over and calmly talked me through the process. While on the one hand he was gentle in his delivery, on the other, he was forceful. He grabbed my hand and torqued it in a way that required me to flip literally heels-over-head. He made it clear that I *was* going to commit to the fall. Over I went ... and it was painless for the first time. As we often find, as it was in this case, my fear of getting hurt actually created an environment with the greatest opportunity for me to be hurt. As the title of this section reflects, fear stifles you in every way.

My final story moves the pendulum even further to the right. As you know, I travel a great deal. And some days, being in the air can be a terrifying experience. When you are on a plane and there are storms all around, with lightning in the clouds on both sides with the plane bouncing up and down so viciously you believe the wings should fall off any minute, these are terrifying moments. When you think you have a chance of dying in the near-term, that fear all but paralyzes you and it is not uncommon to find yourself forgetting to breathe as all of your mental capacity is caught up processing the way you feel in that moment.

Regardless of whether I am talking about fear on one extreme (fear of success in my golfing example) or the other (fear of being trapped in a plane that might fall from the sky at any second), the answer is not only the same, but is simple. Face your fear and accept it. It is as though fear is a virus, constantly coursing through our veins and waiting for the first sign of weakness so that it can instantly activate and take over. The problem is that fear tends to stifle positive and effec-tive emotional, physiological, and intellectual responses. In fact, fear often instigates the most unacceptable and dangerous responses. So, when I am on one of my plane trips from hell, bouncing in the sky, though I know this might sound counterintuitive, the only way for me to control the fear is to accept the outcome that I so much want to avoid. As soon as I have a mental conversation with myself that I very well could die in the next few minutes, the fear instantly dissolves away and my head becomes clear again. When I was having trouble committing to the wheel fall, with John counting down to throw me, I accepted the fact that I might get hurt and focused on what I needed to do. When I have those moments of absurd thinking that the world around me might crater, I accept the fact that it could happen and if it does, I will deal with what is actually coming at me at that time. When I am playing golf and have that negative thought about my swing, I say to myself, "what kind of swing would I take if I were *not* afraid" which gets my mind focused on what I need to be doing. In each case, when fear is creeping in or taking over, I take a deep breath, I embrace the fear, and then clear my mind and think about what I need to be doing right then.

I am reminded of a great classic film called *Twelve O'clock High*. I used it for years as part of the training in my leadership classes. It is a true story about World War II, depicting when the Americans decided to start bombing at 9,000 feet instead of 19,000 feet. The B-17's were not able to inflict the destruction necessary at 19,000 feet in their bombing runs, and to make matters worse, they were taking heavy casualties at that altitude as well. The thought of flying at 9,000 feet was terrifying because they were so much closer to enemy fire. Suffice it to say that the bomber groups were not happy with the orders and did not want to fly at that altitude. I was surprised the first time I saw the movie when Gregory Peck, playing the role of the general that took over a failing bomber squadron that had just been assigned this more difficult mission, gathered his men and told them the following:

> We are in a war, a shooting war, and we've got to fight. And some of us have got to die. I'm not trying to tell you not to be afraid. Fear is normal. But stop worrying about it and about yourselves. Stop making plans. Forget about going home. Consider yourselves already dead.

This is certainly not what I would ever want to hear from my boss, but the message is the same one that I have been sharing above. When you accept the fact that your worst fears can come true, fear immediately loses its grip on you and your mind is instantly freed up to think and respond more decisively, clearly, and effectively to the situation at hand. Don't let fear take your momentum away any longer. Its only power is in the possibility of something bad happening, and with acceptance of that as a possibility, you can easily regain your momentum and keep moving towards your goals.

Assess yourself on your management of fear. Circle how you feel you are doing. On this subject, I:

Need a lot of work	Need a little work	Am okay	Feel good where I am

What fear is stifling you? How is fear taking momentum away from the objectives you are trying to achieve? What changes should you be making to take control of your fears so that you can start regaining your momentum again?

_____

_____

_____

Duty: a Tough Hurdle to Overcome

In my opinion, most people are rarely driven by just their own desires. Rather, they are influenced heavily by the desires and expectations of those around them as well as by the roles they fill (as I briefly touched on in the introduction to this book). Duty is synonymous with words like responsibility and obligation—and the thesaurus offers the phrase "what you have to do." Duty has intellectual and emotional ties to your value systems too. Therefore, to defy one's duty is to default on one's values. Someone's sense of duty can be so strong that he or she will not even consider changing a plan or embracing a different idea, regardless of how dire the consequences might be. Just consider the secret service agents who guard the President—it is their duty to jump in front of a bullet to protect the president. When duty to your job trumps self-preservation, that makes it clear how strong this emotion this can be.

Who wrote your guide book that details what your duties are as a parent, spouse, teacher, child, and so on? What is your duty to your country? What is your duty to your job or other owners in your company? You might have a sense of duty that you need to "pull your own weight" in whatever you do, or that you should provide a minimum specific level of care for your loved ones. The expectations go on and on. The problem with duty is that we rarely challenge its origin or the validity of this ingrained mindset. When you have a sense of duty about something, it often converts to a response akin to "stubbornness on steroids."

I remember the many discussions with Michaelle about her quitting her job at IBM so that she could earn her doctorate. I told her on numerous occasions that she could quit any time she wanted and go back to school. Being very pragmatic and practical, she would ask, "How are we going to make this work, especially financially?" Being the more risk inclined between the two of us, I would say, "We'll make it work." My wife would then, unbeknownst to me, start to think thoughts like:

- Bill is self-employed and his income is erratic;
- It's tough to make it in small business today and I don't want to put extra pressure on him;
- I have a good income with a great company. I should just stop being selfish;
- I might not be accepted into a Ph.D. program anyway;
- I am not comfortable introducing this kind of drama and change into our lives;
- What if we make this change and I am not happy as a professor ... how could I live with that? And so much more.

No matter how many times I would say to Michaelle, "Do what you want to do and we'll be fine," she would get caught up in some kind of internal duty dialogue that would quickly kill the idea. One day, she went to lunch with a good friend of hers, who was also a previous partner of mine as well as a previous colleague of ours at IBM. After lunch with Trudy, Michaelle walked in, looked at me, and said, "I'm going to start applying to schools this week, and if I am accepted into a Ph.D. program I like, I am going to quit IBM!" My reaction was one of complete surprise. I wasn't against the idea, but what could have changed between that morning (when the subject hadn't been mentioned in months, maybe even a year) and after lunch that motivated this dramatic shift in conviction? When I asked, "What happened at lunch?" Michaelle replied, "Trudy told me that I deserved the chance to get my Ph.D.!" I responded, "I have been telling you that I would support that change for years." She responded, "Yes, but I did not believe you. And I thought it was selfish of me to put that kind of pressure on you to provide for us. I felt it was my duty to pull an equal financial weight in our relationship. But Trudy told me that your being self-employed was the best job in the world because you get to do exactly what you want to do every day. Trudy told me it was my turn now!" So, here was a case where my wife's sense of duty was so overwhelming that it was stopping her from giving real consideration to her Desire. It wasn't me, it was not about her ability, or even her comfort with risk, but rather that she didn't feel she had permission. Once Michaelle processed her conversation with Trudy, she gave a higher priority to her evaluation of "fair" (in other words, it was her turn to pursue her dream as I was already pursing mine) and lowered the priority of her definition of duty regarding the contribution she should make to our family. Once this reprioritization occurred, permission was instantly granted. She never looked back, not for a moment, and she earned her Ph.D. about four years later.

Assess yourself on whether duty is a hurdle to overcome. Circle how you feel you are doing. On this subject, I:

Need a lot of work	Need a little work	Am okay	Feel good where I am

What sense of duty is holding you back from pursuing what you desire? Where might you want to consider reprioritizing so that your sense of duty falls more in line with what you really want?

_____

_____

_____

Guilt Is One of the Most Damaging Emotional Obstacles You Throw in Front of Yourself

When I talk about guilt and duty, the examples I share can sound similar. However, the distinction to me is that duty is what you feel before you make a decision or take an action, and guilt is what you feel afterward. For example, I feel a sense of duty to protect my daughter, and I would feel guilty if she were hurt badly because I would imagine everything I should have done to better protect her (even if what I imagined would be unreasonable to expect). I believe guilt is one of the most damaging of all of our emotions because it runs so deep and is so well hidden that it is difficult to surface and address. As overachievers, we frequently have guilt that we did not live up to something, whether that be guilt that we have not been a good enough partner or parent or spouse, guilt that we did not live up to our parents' expectations, guilt that we should be better people, guilt that we are too selfish ... I could go on with examples for pages. I believe guilt is the single biggest product we manufacture in the United States because it is easy for us to feel guilty about almost anything. So, an important step to take when trying to regain your momentum is to stop comparing yourself to some idealized self-image; in this way every action you take or decision you make isn't perceived as a shortcoming in your performance or character. As soon as you stop this comparing, you will be able to see the world and your choices more clearly.

After Michaelle and I started simplifying our lives about two decades ago, we spent some quality time thinking about how we wanted to spend our future. One of the reasons Michaelle wanted to be a professor was to have summers off so that she could hike, play golf, read more books, relax, and so on. When we decided to build our new careers around this work-life balance idea, it didn't take long for us to come up with the idea to buy a condo in the mountains. However, we were a long way from being financially positioned to do that. One of the first tests we came up with was to spend several weeks in the area we were considering, to see if we really liked it as much as we thought we would. Well, that ended up being a no-brainer test. We loved it. Then we put a plan together to manage our finances so that over the next five years, we would be in a position to handle the purchase of second home. In 1998 we were able to purchase a townhome in the mountains, and in 2000, we sold that and bought a home.

Now, let's get back to the topic of guilt. Despite our longtime planning and saving, after we had achieved our goal, I found it difficult to enjoy my time off. The reason: I felt guilty! I had two partners and several staff back in Austin that were working away. We made some adjustments to my earnings for my time away and no one ever challenged that I was not earning my pay. In fact my partners never mentioned that I shouldn't go and actually never said a thing but "have a great time and we will see you at the end of summer." It didn't matter. My sense of duty, even though I worked about the same number of hours in the mountains as I did in Austin, actually got in the way of my happiness because I felt guilty about having such a great time while my partners were toiling away at the office. Ultimately, in 1999, I split with my partners, not because of anything they did wrong, but because I couldn't let go of the guilt I felt for following my plan. Here was a classic case of my running from myself rather than learning to deal with my emotions.

What guilt is holding you back from pursing the life you want? What is it that you feel you don't have the right to do, or that requesting it would be selfish? Give yourself permission. Here are a couple of thoughts I often consider, and remind others about, to help them work through this:

> *The most wonderful gift you can give those who love and care about you is for you to be happy!*

> *The best way to serve others and make a positive contribution to their lives is to find a way to be happy living yours.*

Assess yourself on whether your guilt needs to be better managed.
Circle how you feel you are doing. On this subject, I:

Need a lot of work	Need a little work	Am okay	Feel good where I am

What feeling of guilt is holding you back from achieving whatever objective you have in mind? Where might guilt have more control over your decisions and actions than it should?

_____

_____

_____

Understand That the Road to Wisdom Is Often Paved With Failure

Besides guilt, overachievers seem to have a real problem with the idea of failure, which is why it comes up in so many different forms throughout the book. How does this attitude toward failure manifest itself? Well, in business, as with life, we are taught by society that to be considered a worthy and successful human being, we must "grab for the brass ring" or buy into the idea that "winning is everything." And clichés like "anything other than first doesn't count" are used to motivate people into obtaining "the right perspective." This has created some self-destructive and dysfunctional attitudes toward winning.

As a backlash to the baby boomers' competitive nature, which was nurtured by an oversupply of workers and an undersupply of jobs, many of them decided that they did not want their kids growing up with such an emphasis on winning. To take the heat off of their kids as they began to play sports and compete, some decided to perpetuate the idea that "everyone is a winner just for trying." This morphed into ceremonies at the end of a sports season when everyone was handed a trophy regardless of the team's actual record, attitude of the players, efforts of the individuals, skill of the group, and so on. This solution of avoiding the idea of failure, or pretending that those who lost actually won, is easily more damaging in my opinion as the idea they were running from.

The lesson that we all need to be learning and constantly reminding ourselves of is that winning and losing both play important roles in our personal development. Although the winners typically get to enjoy the spotlight and the spoils of victory, the losers gain important experience, perspective, and awareness of the skills needing improvement to be more competitive the next time around. The funny thing is, while the baby boomer parents were trying to take the pressure off of their kids to win, they were actually reinforcing the importance of winning rather than teaching the more critical lesson about the value of failure and the personal growth that can occur from this learning experience.

Unfortunately, the pedestal that we put under winners is bad enough, but the disrespect we cast upon the losers is what really damages an individual's ability to learn and grow. Because the idea of failing is so oppressive, it restricts our willingness to venture into unfamiliar areas. The problem is that venturing into unfamiliar areas is how we gain experience and knowledge, which are foundational to how we improve.

> It's funny that being wise is considered so admirable, yet the road to wisdom, which is paved with failure, is to be avoided at all costs.

This reminds me of an old story. It went like this:

> A successful businessman was interviewed and asked, "What has made you so successful?" He replied, "Making good decisions!" "How are you able to make so many good decisions?" the interviewer rebutted. The businessman answered, "My experience." The interviewer questioned, "How did you gain your experience?" He answered, "From bad decisions."

The reality is that growth occurs when we end up on the wrong side of a decision and use that experience to learn. When we make mistakes, we often dig into the situation to uncover what information misdirected or confused our decision making process. We first want to determine why it wasn't our fault, and for most, we eventually move on to identifying the warning signs that will help us avoid making this same mistake again. For those that are not content until they find someone to blame, all I can say is that this determination is sad to me. Blaming others is a way to pretend you are not an active player in your own life. Yes, someone else may also be at fault. However, that doesn't mitigate the fact that you played a role in whatever outcome you experienced. I am reminded of my first investment experience in the stock market. Here is the way I remember it:

> Early in the life of the personal computer, I bought shares in an IPO from BPI, a successful Austin, Texas PC-based accounting software developer, for $12 a share. Within a short time, the stock went to about $17 dollars. I bought some more. It went up into the twenties. I bought some more. It went to around $27. I bought some more. I clearly remember my arrogance when I mentioned to Michaelle that I thought I should quit IBM so I could play the stock market full time since I was clearly an investment genius. I commented, "just imagine what I could do

if this were my daily job!" Well, fortunately, she was smart enough not to take me up on my offer. Soon, the stock dropped to $24 per share. Realizing that in my 20's I might not have been exposed to all of the applicable knowledge in the world on this subject, I called my broker and asked for her assistance. She quizzed me about the corporation and I told her I believed in BPI's product. As someone working with technology and accounting, I knew there was a long-term need for the product and was impressed with its functionality. So, she suggested that I "buy some more stock and average down." While this seemed to be an odd thing to do, I was told that by following this strategy, I could get back into the gain column sooner because I would be averaging down the cost of my investment. Therefore, when the stock rebounded, I would be in a position to make more money at a lower price. Then the stock fell to $17. And yes, I bought some more and averaged down. The bottom line is that I sold all of my stock when Computer Associates forced a buyout at a $1.38 per share.

Mistakes heighten our learning experiences. While my BPI stock was going up, I wasn't learning, I was just congratulating myself for my raw talent. It was only when the stock started falling and I kept making the wrong decisions that I began to try to understand more about how the market worked as well as how to keep this from happening again. It wasn't my stock broker's fault for suggesting that I buy more and average down, it was my fault for not understanding what I was doing. It was my fault for being so naïve as I invested my money. It was my fault for allowing my ego to get the better of me in my decision making because I could have cut and run with a nice profit multiple times along the way.

Since one of the messages here is that the road to wisdom is often paved with failure, let's take a look at how I am defining this. Failure definitions are as diverse as our world population. To some, it is merely "being caught" doing something wrong. In other words, as long as the mistake or failure wasn't acknowledged, then it wasn't one. This is a common perspective for people playing in organized sports. For example, in basketball, when the player I guarded took a shot, as soon as the ball was out of his hands I would block out (turning, backing into him and wrapping my arms around him to keep him from a possible rebound). Often, I did this in a way that was far more restrictive than the rules allowed. However, the only time that mattered was if a foul was called. Otherwise, my actions were viewed as "doing my job" because I was able to push the boundary of the rules in favor of my team. However, this type of approach works both ways. I remember in one game, I aggressively blocked out my opponent multiple times in a row as he missed each of his shots. By the fourth time down the floor, after another errant long shot, I had the luxury of becoming intimate with the four knuckles of his fist as the shooter unleashed a round house to the side of my face. Guess what? The referee didn't call that either because my opponent was smart enough to do it when no one was looking. Needless to say, I was less aggressive for the rest of the game. So, breaking the rules or making mistakes, to some, doesn't count unless you get caught.

While "being caught" is one extreme, the other—expanded to unreasonable heights—goes back to an idea introduced above that "anything other than being first or being the best" constitutes failure. What a ridiculous framework to try to work within. Can everyone be first if they work hard enough? The answer is an unequivocal no. We can't control who is the best or who is first. All we can do is the best we can; if we win or happen to be the best there is at that moment in time— that is a fantastic bonus. Consider this true story:

> Little Billy, about nine years old (not me, but I would be happy if it had been), trained in martial arts every week. One day, he approached his martial arts Master and asked permission to miss several months of training. Billy wanted to concentrate on preparing for an upcoming track meet. During this time, Billy trained hard and felt he was ready for the big race.
>
> The starting gun was fired and they were off. Billy ran as fast as he ever had, but finished inches behind the winner. For days after the event, Billy sat in his room, crying, feeling discouraged and beaten.
>
> Not sure how to get Billy motivated again, his mother dragged him to the martial arts training facility to see if his Master could help. When the Master asked what was wrong, Billy could barely comment through his tears. Once the whole story had been told, here is the conversation that took place:
>
> **Master Instructor**: "Billy, pretend that the boy who won didn't show up because he hurt his leg the day before the race. Because he wouldn't have been there, you would have been the fastest runner. You would have come in first. Would that make you feel better?"
>
> **Billy**: "Yes!"
>
> **Master Instructor**: (Grinning as he put his arms around Billy) "Did you train hard and do your best?"
>
> **Billy**: Nodded yes.
>
> **Master Instructor**: "Remember this. You do not become a true champion because of someone else's failure. You also are not a loser because of someone else's success. You become a champion by doing the best you can with your abilities every day, which has nothing to do with how anyone else performs."

Unfortunately, many, much older than little Billy, find themselves falling into this same trap. Why? Because the final outcome becomes more important than the effort, the experience, or the journey. In corporate America, we give more credit to people who stay long hours than those who accomplish a great deal. We bestow rewards to those who merely stay within their known limits and operate mistake free rather than those who try to extend their knowledge and experience limits and fail. We empower our employees so that they will take action, yet we punish them when their decisions are wrong or inconsistent with our own. We have a system which expects consistent superior quality and performance, but does not allow the personal growth necessary in order to achieve it. It is sad, but most of us, at some time, fall into the "little Billy trap" and judge people solely by how they finish the race and do little to recognize the incremental steps people take every day to improve themselves and do the best that they can.

I believe it is essential that you learn to give yourself permission to fail, permission to learn from failure, permission to work through failure, and permission to enjoy the growth experience created from failing. And if you are going to compare yourself to anyone, the only fair comparison to make is whether you have generated the attitude and effort to make yourself better, faster, or stronger than you were.

Assess yourself on your comfort with embracing failure. Circle how you feel you are doing. On this subject, I:

Need a lot of work	Need a little work	Am okay	Feel good where I am

What do you need to do to change the way you feel about failure and embrace it rather than run from or avoid it? Where might the fear of failure be holding you back from what is important to you?

_____

_____

_____

Time Passes Anyway

"Time passes anyway" is a phrase commonly tossed around at John's school. It is the reminder that change comes from doing the work and therefore we need to make every workout count. Days will pass—30, 60, 90—in what feels like the blink of an eye, and when you make every day count, before you know it, you will be a lot better. Whether you use your days well, or simply throw them away, know that time passes anyway and that time can never be reclaimed!

Going back to my story about Michaelle's desire to earn her Ph.D., one of the reasons she also expressed early on as to why she shouldn't make a career change was because she was too old. She also said, "Why should I go to school to get my Ph.D. this late in my career? No one is looking for a new professor at my age." Well, she was clearly wrong on both counts. Remember, time passes anyway, whether or not you take action to achieve your desires. When she first mentioned earning her doctorate, she was in her early 30s and she thought she was too old then. She ended up making the change in her early 40s. However, if Michaelle were 60 and this challenge was important to her from a self-fulfillment perspective, then she wouldn't have been too old then, either. Age doesn't matter—it is about doing whatever makes you feel happy or successful. While it was another four years before she began working as a professor, she has been living that dream for almost 15 years and is right now starting phased-retirement over the next 5 years.

Look at it this way. Would you voluntarily go to prison and live there for 10 years? Of course not! Why would anyone confine themselves for 10 years doing something they do not want to do? So I ask you, unless you are doing exactly what you want to do right now, why are you giving up your freedom and voluntarily staying in your own personal jail? Time passes anyway. If you don't take action now, if you don't rethink your priorities now, months or even years will pass by without your ever putting your hands on the steering wheel guiding your life. If you act now, within a few short weeks, months, or years, rather than putting off the goal you want to attain, you will be either closer to or have already achieved it. Instead of lamenting changes you need to make in the future, you will be able to relax, reflect, and enjoy the transformation you have already experienced.

Assess yourself on your awareness that time passes anyway as you make choices. Circle how you feel you are doing. On this subject, I:

Need a lot of work	Need a little work	Am okay	Feel good where I am

Time passes anyway, so don't let it pass without taking full advantage of every minute of it. What am I currently putting my life on hold for or waiting for it to pass before I move on? What do I want to do but feel time has already passed me by? Because time passes anyway, what I am going to do differently?

_____

_____

_____

Don't Let Worry Consume You

Worry is an instinctive response that is meant to surface an issue or problem that needs attention. It is an internal alarm system saying, "Danger, Danger, Will Robinson, Danger" (okay, you got me ... a quote from *Lost in Space*, a mid-60s TV series). Like so many of our psychological and physiological responses, too much or too little of this emotion can be equally negative. If you don't ever worry, then you might get caught off guard regarding something you could have easily prepared for. On the other hand, too much worry is like too much adrenalin: your body will just wear itself out by constantly processing it. Worry is often manifested in a barrage of negative thoughts and emotions that steal your energy, create a cloud of doom over your life, and can be a disabling force.

Worry can be good when it is a thought that you instantly consider, manage, respond to, and then calm. However, while a little bit of worrying might be positive, it won't take long before this act turns very negative. When you regularly find yourself worrying, then you have allowed this internal response system to get out of hand and move from being a good survival tool to one that can eventually control your life. Worry is a form of fear. And just like fear, the best way to control it is to accept the possible outcome you are concerned about, and then do what you can right now to improve your chances of avoiding that situation.

Worrying can be a valuable informational tool, but when those thoughts start, keep the worry in check and use it in a positive way by doing the following:

1. Recognize what it is you are actually worrying about. What is the root cause driving these emotions?

2. Accept the idea that what you are considering could occur.

3. Ask yourself if there is anything you should be doing right now to alter the course of this possibly damaging situation.

4. If the answer to question 3 is "yes," then take a moment to identify what you are going to do and when.

5. If the answer to question 3 is "no," then clean your mind through a quick meditation and let those negative thoughts go.

Using these steps, you can manage your amount of worrying instead of allowing it to manage you. This accountability of knowing that you are responsible for controlling this mental process will allow you to continue moving on your path rather than becoming a wreck along the way. As Bobby McFerrin simplifies in his hit song, "In your life expect some trouble. When you worry you make it double. Don't Worry! Be Happy!"

Assess yourself on your worry management. Circle how you feel you are doing. On this subject, I:

Need a lot of work	Need a little work	Am okay	Feel good where I am

What am I worrying about? What can I do so that worry is a useful tool and doesn't consume me?

_____

_____

_____

Your Perception Will Shape Your Experiences

Your perception of what you expect will actually shape what you experience. Let's consider a few common perspective variations like "scarcity versus abundance," "one right answer versus many right answers," "opportunity versus threats," "easy versus struggle," "success versus failure," "happiness versus sadness" just to name a few. With each of these, there is a continuum between one extreme and the other, and depending on where your outlook falls on that continuum, your perspective—that filter—will shape the way you interpret every experience.

For example, if we think there is a limited availability of something we want, studies have proven that we will act more hastily and less thoughtfully as we try to procure whatever it is while supplies last. Salespeople often try to invoke the feeling of "scarcity" to create urgency around a decision they want you to make. My experience is that rarely is there real scarcity. For example, let's consider that after months of looking, you finally find the perfect house, but the owners won't sell it for a price you feel is reasonable. The feeling of scarcity would motivate most people to pay too much or more than they can afford. Why? Because they feel that if they don't buy that specific house, another opportunity like it will never present itself again. I used to be easily manipulated by thoughts such as these. Fortunately, through my many years of experience being led around by the nose by others more worldly, to stay with the same analogy, I found that there are many great houses to be found. Sometimes you had to look a little harder, sometimes you had a wait a little longer, but ideal houses were always there, or about to come onto the market. I was able to shift my perspective from looking at everything through the filter of scarcity to seeing everything through a filter of abundance. When you approach life with the idea of abundance, there is no reason to overreact by purchasing the last one, because even if it is the last one, there will be other alternatives that will come along that will make you just as happy, if not happier.

I am not suggesting that you should put off whatever you are trying to accomplish to wait for the next best thing. I am simply stating that you almost always have alternatives. There really will be another "perfect house," maybe at an even better price; a different great car that better fits your wish list; a new employee with stronger skills for the same salary; or an alternative business idea with even greater potential. As I look back on my life, some of the things that I truly wanted and did everything possible to make happen ended up great ... but an equal number of those situations turned out fairly marginal. Even more surprising, some of the things that I experienced that seemed terrible at the time actually created very positive changes in my life.

Many of the seemingly disparate perspectives mentioned above can also link together. In other words, one perspective may position you for the next. For example

- the belief in scarcity can lead to the idea that there is just one right answer so you have to find it,
- which can lead to the idea that you have to take advantage of every good opportunity because it might be your last one,
- which can lead to the concept that life should always be a struggle because everyone wants what you want so you have to continuously fight for the few good things,
- which can lead to the idea that success and happiness are rare, so one shouldn't expect to experience either for long,
- which can lead to the idea you are better off expecting bad things to happen so that you won't be constantly disappointed, and the cycle continues.

Let me walk through this list and share with you why each is sending you down a rabbit hole.

As a consultant, I used to believe it was my job to find the one right answer to my client's problems. I believed that while there were plenty of solutions, there was truly only one right one. I tried to find the approach that statistically gave us the greatest chance of success.

However, what I often found was that (1) I didn't always have enough information to really identify that best answer, (2) people make or break ideas—so it was not as much about what might work as it was about what the client believed in and would support, and (3) that there is no shortage of good ideas and right answers, each with different strengths and weaknesses.

I think there is an abundance of opportunity. Rather than having to make one opportunity work because it might be your last, I now consider whether the current opportunity is good enough to tie me up to the point that I won't be able to consider the new opportunities presenting themselves every day.

As for life being a struggle, certainly you will encounter struggles throughout your life. However, there are people I have encountered that simply gravitate toward struggle—they look for it, want to hang on to it, and it seems as if somehow they are comforted by the misery of it. As you approach whatever you are trying to achieve, know that while some struggle should be expected, it doesn't have to become your norm unless you are looking for it to be.

Success and happiness are not rare. If you are like most of the people I know, you experience successes every day, and you have moments of happiness all of the time. The question is whether you are writing off those successes and worrying away your happiness. The problem with success is that it is relative. Do you remember the story about little Billy's disappointment in coming in second at his track meet? He wasn't comparing his race results against his previous performances—he was making the common mistake of comparing his results against those of others. The other common mistake we make after a successful action or encounter is to assume that anyone could have accomplished what we just did. As I discussed earlier, it is difficult to feel successful when you are constantly ratcheting up your goals and setting new targets long before you reach even the first ones. These kinds of thought processes are self-destructive because they continually reinforce messages that you are unsuccessful, when in fact, you are achieving success every day. So, don't write off your successes—accept the idea that it is okay for you to enjoy them.

I also see happiness washed away just like our successes. For example, in those moments when you find yourself in a happy place, if you instantly start trying to hold on to those feelings or begin wondering when those feeling will go away, you will effectively worry your happiness away. You have to enjoy the feelings as they come along. Don't try to contain them. Don't try to analyze them. Just feel them. Remember El Yunque: the joy was there all along ... I was just too busy to see it on the way up. Thankfully, I came to my senses on my way down.

This leads me to my personal favorite. "If I expect things to go bad, then I won't be disappointed when they do. If they end up better than I expected, well, that's when I will be happy." This mindset is rooted in ideas like (1) there is a scarcity of success available; (2) falling short of expectation in any way is failure; and (3) a failure of an act should translate to failure as a human being which should be embraced by shame and embarrassment. This way of thinking—"I want to avoid disappointment at all cost"—just baffles me.

Last summer, I was playing golf with a friend and we got into this exact discussion. He wants to hit a good golf shot, he hopes to hit a good shot, but he expects to hit a bad shot. When I asked him why in the world he would think this way, his response was, "As long as I don't allow myself to think I will hit a good shot, I am not as disappointed when I don't because I was not expecting to anyway. And when I do hit a good shot, because I don't allow myself to think I will, I am just that much happier when I do. This approach keeps me from getting too disappointed when I play golf." So, here is what I heard when he explained this to me.

> I am choosing the mental state of being unhappy for almost the entire round of golf. This way, if I hit a bad shot (something to be unhappy about), because I am already unhappy, it is no big deal. And if I hit a good shot (something to be happy about), because I am normally in an unhappy state, I experience a greater amount of joy in that moment. Then, I reset my emotions and go back to being unhappy until the next positive event occurs, all to avoid becoming too unhappy.

If you do the math, it becomes clear that it is absurd to voluntarily think this way, unless of course your objective is to be generally unhappy almost all of the time. In a round of golf, often about four and a half hours, we are actually only in the process of hitting a golf ball for about 20% of that time (about 50 minutes). For the remaining approximately three and a half hours of the golf round, we are getting to our ball, trying to find our ball, waiting for someone else to hit a ball, and so forth. So, why wouldn't you at least choose to be happy for this three and a half hour period regardless of how the remaining time goes?

Here is the sad part. After playing many rounds of golf with my friend, I can tell you that his philosophy isn't really protecting him from anything because, based on my observations, when he hits a bad shot, whether he was mentally prepared to do so or not, his frustration level spikes. Whether you succeed or fail, whether an effort turns out good or bad, during that moment of realization, you will feel some spike in your emotions. So, if the emotional surge is going to occur anyway, positive or negative, doesn't it make sense to try to be happy all of the rest of the time? As well, when you prepare yourself mentally to fail, because your mind is processing those thoughts and likely creating physical responses to match them (like excess tension), you increase the odds that you will in fact fail. Don't prepare yourself to fail ... if it happens, deal with it, then forget about it, then get up and get ready to go again.

Here is an old joke that I have heard many times that really sums up how your perspective can shape your world:

> A young couple had twin boys about the age of five. Though they were alike in so many ways, in one way they were vastly different. Joey, a generally melancholy kid, was commonly disappointed by life and would often succumb to the negative view of whatever was going on around him. Bobby, on the other hand, was almost always happy. He had a very bright outlook on life and always expected good things to come his way. Mom and dad were a little concerned that both boys' views of life were out of balance, so they decided a "teaching moment" was in order.
>
> On the boys' sixth birthday, they wanted both to experience life as the other saw it. So, while both were in school, the parents filled Joey's room with new toys knowing that this would help him realize that unbelievably good things can happen. And to help Bobby see that life does have it disappointments, they dumped a large pile of manure in the corner of his room as his present. Upon arriving home, both boys, as they did every day, went to their rooms to change out of their school clothes. After waiting about 20 minutes, the parents decided to check in and see how the life-lessons were unfolding. As they peered into Joey's room, his parents noticed him sitting amongst his toys staring off in space. Surprised not to see him frantically playing running from new toy to new toy, they asked, "What's wrong?" Joey replied, "I'm bored. These toys are nice, but I was hoping for a new train set. And besides, my friends are not here to play with me." Disappointed that their experiment didn't work with Joey, they went to open the door to Bobby's room fully expecting him to be crying over his very smelly new environment. As they got closer, they heard Bobby laughing with noises that sounded like he had to be tossing himself around the room. When they opened the door, they saw Bobby half buried in his giant pile of dung. They pulled him out and said, "Bobby, what is going on here?" How can you be so happy with this smelly manure in your room? Bobby smiled as he got ready to start digging again and said, "There has to be a pony in here somewhere."

We have all dug through a pile of dung or two in our lives. Like Bobby, we have a choice in the way we view that effort. You can spend your time looking for what is missing, thinking about how your situation falls short of expectation, or expecting the worst. Or, you can dig through life with enthusiasm, hoping to find your pony. Whether there is a pony buried beneath the manure is totally out of your control, and you will experience whatever emotions that arise once the reality of your situation is known. But I would recommend that because the vast majority of the time in our lives is spent in anticipation or in route of an expectation, choose "happy" as your default feeling, choose "hope" as your default outlook, and choose "resilience" as your response to whatever happens. Deal with disappointment when it comes, but rather than look at it as some deep dark pit you have to climb out of, just think of it as a life experience that will only make you better, faster, stronger, and smarter! And recognize that your perception of the world has a dramatic effect on the world that will actually take shape around you.

Assess yourself on creating your world. Circle how you feel you are doing. On this subject, I:

Need a lot of work	Need a little work	Am okay	Feel good where I am

What can I do to change my perspective so that I more frequently choose happy, hope, and resilience instead of scary, struggle, and disappointment? How am I getting stuck because I won't allow myself to consider that there might be a pony in the pile of dung I am dealing with?

_____

_____

_____

"What You *Are* Thinking" Wrap-Up

We need self-acceptance that as human beings we are emotional, have faults, are regularly scared, will make mistakes, are very self-critical, expect more from ourselves at times than is reasonable, and more. We need to accept the fact that we will commonly sabotage or undermine our own efforts, sometimes consciously, often subconsciously. When we find our psychological and physiological energy heading down one of these destructive paths, rather than pile on and beat ourselves up even more, we need to accept that these detours are both expected and predictable so that we can quickly refocus on more constructive responses.

Know that past successes don't guarantee future performance. And know that past joy does not ensure future happiness. Constantly self-monitor what you are thinking and how our body and mind are responding to all of the hurdles you put in your own way. Remember that, at times, you can be your own worst enemy and therefore you need to be prepared to constantly forgive yourself. The sooner you see the reality of being off path or losing momentum towards your objectives, the quicker you can examine what you are thinking, determine what you need to let go of, and start moving again closer to what you actually desire.

Now that you have read through the "What You *Are* Thinking" chapter, several ideas may have come to mind that will help you regain your momentum and get you back on your path towards whatever you are looking to achieve. If not, just keep reading because the next chapter, "What You *Are* Doing" might raise some awareness as to actions you should be taking.

Once you have found a technique that will help you let go of something, consider whether the appropriate action to get you jump started again would be to replan, reprioritize or reaffirm. As you can see from the following flowchart, your choice—how you change your thinking—will determine what course of action is best for you (do you resolve the issue and return to the Try (Work)-Evaluate loop, or do you need to replan).

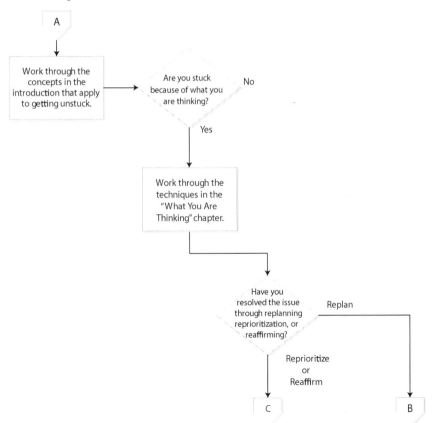

Chapter 6
What You *Are* Doing

You are now at the final leg of the Process. To be here, you had to kick out of the Try (Work)-Evaluate loop because you were either feeling unsuccessful or unhappy about your progress or priorities. This negative evaluation occurs as you are either starting to get stuck or you are already stuck. Since you have already worked through the techniques covered in chapter 5, "What You *Are* Thinking," it's time for us to walk through the other side of this evaluation which is "What You *Are* Doing" The techniques covered in this chapter should help you find ways to get unstuck from what you are doing so that you can once again start regaining momentum towards whatever goal you are trying to accomplish.

Tenacity and Persistence, Friend or Foe?

My dad, who died in December of 2008, was my best friend and someone I will always admire for the life he led and the values he lived. I wish he were alive today to read this book because I know he would be smiling and chuckling often. I also believe he would have truly enjoyed reading about my exploration and discovery, even in this section as I challenge one of his foundational teachings.

From an early age, my father taught me that tenacity and persistence were two of the greatest tools for success. His belief was that those who achieve do so by staying focused, doing the work, and tenaciously and persistently staying the course to overcome all obstacles. It was as if he believed that everyone had the same basic skills, so the only real determining success factor was who could overcome—time and time again—the obstacles put in front of them. To him, at the end of the day, the winners were always the ones left standing—those persistent long enough to be survivors.

My dad grew up in the depression and he also had a tough start in life: his father died when he was 12 and his family struggled throughout his teenage years to put food on the table. He used to tell me stories of how he would walk to school every day 5 miles in the snow, uphill both ways (I think every parent tells that one). He joined the military early and fought in two wars, including the big one. It would certainly make sense that his philosophies were rooted and shaped by these major events. And though I agree with the premise that tenacity and persistence are important tools for success, I believe they can easily become drivers of chaos and struggle, and eventually a weakness. Let me explain.

I do believe in the power of tenacity and persistence ... to a point. You can't run from every obstacle in your way because life regularly puts them in front of you everywhere you go. My experiences as an athlete immediately come to mind because if I had been uncomfortable getting up, dusting myself off and trying again after falling short, I would never have been able to do anything that required much hand-eye coordination or flexibility. I would definitely tell you that tenacity and persistence have clearly been my friends.

I will also tell you they are major foes as well. Too many times, these two qualities lock your mind into a detrimental way of thinking. In other words, we get so focused at breaking down a door that we don't just turn the knob and open it, or we don't look for the easy alternative to go through an open window instead. During the last two decades, Michaelle and I have adopted a different philosophy regarding the use of these tools. While we are prepared and plan on using them when attempting to achieve any goal or objective, we monitor closely for their over-use. If it seems that the only way to make something work is to constantly call on persistence and tenacity to force it, we regroup and make sure we still believe in the desire and plan we are following. I don't want to get too new-agey on you, but as we looked back over our successes, our marginal successes, and our failures, we came to the conclusion that when we were on the right track in our approach and goals, our effort and accomplishment came together pretty easily. That doesn't mean that we didn't have to overcome hurdles or experience failures along the way, but overall, things seem to fall into place.

On the other hand, there have been plenty of times when one of our many theoretically good ideas just wasn't panning out, but due to pure tenacity and persistence, we were able to keep those ideas or initiatives alive. However, in these cases, they were not thriving, but rather on life-support because we should have just let them die. I didn't realize then that we were paying such a high price (in potential lost opportunity) spending so much of our time and resources keeping some of our marginal initiatives from fading away. To be fair, Michaelle realized this long before me because I was unable to see clearly given that I was too busy beating my head against the door trying to open it. But, as she so often does, she finally convinced me to step back and look at our situation from a different perspective. What I realized was that tenacity and persistence can easily get intertwined with ego and vanity, and when that happens, bad things are about to come your way.

Our second ladies' clothing store was a good example of this. We opened up a dress shop called "Suited for Success," a professional women's clothing store, over three decades ago in casual Austin, Texas. After years of operating a single store about 8 miles from downtown, we were approached by a well-known retail consultant who asked us to open a second store in downtown. We were offered an experimental retail space—it was an open area in an office building (we had a little metal fence around it with multiple entry points). This kind of space is common today in airports and in other retail spaces 25 years later, but when we were propositioned, this design was unheard of. However, how could we pass up the huge incentive of free rent for the first year? Even after that first year, our rent would be a percentage of sales with no minimums for several more years. And besides, downtown was where many of the suit-wearing business women worked. I remember talking to Michaelle and saying, "Wow! ... Free rent ... The right audience ... We need to do this!" I didn't ask questions like

- Does this make sense? (We were absentee owners because we both worked full time at other jobs.)
- Do we have the time to manage two stores?
- Do we have the personnel that we can count on and trust to run two stores?
- Do we have the financial resources to keep two stores stocked?

No, I didn't ask those questions because all I could think about was free rent! Anyway, we opened the store and we moved our store manager to the new location thinking we wanted our best person there in order to give this new operation the greatest chance of working. In the end, several years later, not only did that experimental retail space never take off, but the low traffic was so discouraging for our talented store manager that she eventually quit. In addition, the second store spread our resources too thin (we had really nice stuff tied up at a store with no traffic that we could have easily moved at the original store), and our customers at the original store were disappointed that our talented manager was no longer there. To recap, opening the second store was motivated by an attractive lease without regard to our overall plan and the cost of running it (money, time, and skill). The real failing here was continuing in tenacity and persistence. After six months, we knew opening it was a mistake. However, I was not going to let this store fail and therefore beat me. I was going to make it work, whatever it took. So, we kept working harder and spreading ourselves thinner in order for me to prove to myself that opening this store wasn't a bad idea. It was my persistence to stay the course that finally made my wife throw her hands in the air and say, "I'm done being involved." Finally, after trying for multiple years to out-last and out-effort this situation, we ended up closing the downtown store and then a couple of years later we sold the original store because we were just too burned out to try to keep it going.

There are two important concepts I am asking you to consider without having to go through the painful learning curve I did. First, holding on to an idea or opportunity that requires superhuman effort to keep alive only robs you of the time and energy to explore other possibilities, many of them with far greater potential. Second, accept that tenacity and persistence, misapplied, go from being positive qualities to negative ones that can hold you back and keep you from going through the many open windows in front of you right now.

Assess yourself regarding your tenacity and persistence. Circle how you feel you are doing. On this subject, I:

Need a lot of work	Need a little work	Am okay	Feel good where I am

What should you change to leverage tenancy and persistence to work in your favor instead of allowing them to be your albatross? Where in your life are you trying to beat a door down rather than go through the open window?

_____

_____

_____

Tension Impacts Performance

Your best comes through, especially when you are calling upon fine motor skills, when you are relaxed. Too much tension can quickly impact your mental, physical, and emotional acuity. What I am referring to is finding the right level of tension to support performance at a heightened level. The problem is that there is a fine line between tension that pumps you up and tension that starts to drag you down.

There has been a great deal of research on the relationship between arousal (I am referring to this as tension) and performance. The Yerkes-Dodson law, cited in 1908, predicted an inverted-U function between the two. Simply stated, it said "if the task is complex, requiring fine motor skill or intellectual acuity, peak performance will occur when arousal is low. If the task is relatively simple, requiring only gross motor skill and limited intellectual acuity, performance is stimulated by higher levels of arousal." So, with a task like playing golf, which requires fine motor skills, while a little tension might be good, as tension is added, performance will not only go back down, but will eventually tank. The same tension scenario is true in business situations. For example, a little tension will likely make your presentation to a potential client about why he or she should select your firm crisper and more compelling. Too much tension will cloud your mind and make it difficult to communicate your ideas, which could easily culminate in sending the message to your client that you are incompetent. However, if you are performing a task that requires only gross motor skills, like lifting weights, then performance will continue to peak through a higher level of arousal. From personal experience and from years training and coaching others, I think this phenomenon is more like an inverted J than a U. Why? Because as you add tension, your performance will likely drop way below your baseline performance to the point of incompetence.

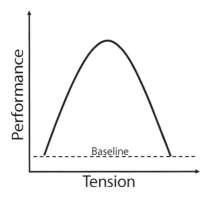

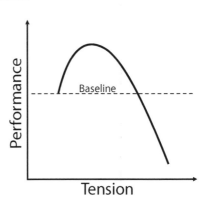

Every time I speak to an audience, whether it is 30 people or 1,000, I am happy when I feel a little anxiety before I go on stage. This little bit of tension keeps me in the present, helps me focus, creates mental clarity and drives me to be prepared. But as the needle rises far above "slight arousal and tension," my level of execution starts to resemble a deer in the headlights level of performance. As we experience in our martial arts training, tension also depletes your energy. Your stamina and endurance shrink exponentially as you hold unnecessary tension in your body. To maintain high energy levels, heighten your performance and improve your stamina, which are all beneficial to supporting your success, health, and happiness, it is important to learn to manage tension.

I remember playing in a golf match my friend set up with one of his acquaintances. I was still in high school at the time. This particular friend was fairly aggressive, so I had a strong feeling he had set up the match to play for money. When I pressed him the morning of the match, he told me that there was a wager on it. He was not surprised when I told him that I didn't want any part of it, so he said "I will cover the bet if we lose and we will share the pot if we win." I told him that I was happy to play, but that I didn't want any part of the money, win or lose. He agreed. So off we went. About five or six holes into the match, I was having fun, enjoying a Saturday game of golf and we were already several holes up. I was surprised about how bad these guys were playing, especially because I knew money was on the line. At the half-way mark, we were well ahead and my partner was very happy. About that time, he came over to me and said something to the order of "I am going to party tonight!" He followed that comment with a status update like, "We are up about $800 right now." Remember that when I was in high school, it was the early 70s. At that time, I had a band that played in the local dance halls over the weekends, and $800 dollars reflected about 10 nights of work for me. When I heard this, something amazing happened. Even though I had nothing to lose or gain, the realization that we were playing for that kind of money was enough to propel me to forget how to swing a golf club. In an instant, I went from making pars and occasional bogies to occasional bogies and regular double bogies. For those non-golfer types reading this, suffice it to say that I went from playing okay to playing badly. Fortunately for my teammate, the guys that were $800 down were far more invested emotionally in protecting their money than I was. With each hole, the pressure for them increased and their performance worsened. In the end, I think my friend took home about $1,500. And no, I didn't take a dime. But I can tell you that tension instantly impacted my performance. I can also assure you that tension was the difference as I watched my opponents' golf games slip from marginal to terrible.

The next time you find yourself in a situation when you need to access your fine motor skills or your intellect, remember to try to relax and constantly look for ways to get rid of the tension and anxiety. When you listen to star athletes talk about their superior performance in a game, they will often comment that at crunch time or game ending moments, everything slows down for them. This is not surprising because they find a place, often called "the zone," where they are calm, relaxed, and confident allowing them at that moment enhanced access to their mental and physical capabilities. By maintaining a relaxed state and minimizing my tension in pressure packed meetings when facilitating or consulting with clients, I can find myself in this same zone where I am able to slow down the conversations in my mind, consider the conflicts and alternatives, and keep the meetings moving in a positive direction.

Once you realize how much tension can impact your performance and your ability to achieve your goals, it makes sense that you will want to learn how to vigilantly monitor for this state change. Whenever you feel your performance starting to drop because your tension or your arousal level is too high, you should instantly put mind and body into a better place. In other words, take a moment to put yourself into a quick meditative state. As I have learned from years of training, breathing is the most direct tool to communicate with and manage your body. So, stay with me and try this. For only two or three minutes, breathe in from your nose and out from your nose and mouth with the tip of your tongue placed gently on the palette just behind your upper front teeth. Then, breathe in and let your diaphragm expand and fill completely with air. When you breathe out, compress all of the air from your diaphragm and then repeat this exercise with nothing else on your mind but concentrating on the sound of your breathing. Try to make each breathe a little deeper with each cycle being a little longer. Think about making the transitions between breathing in and out negligible (you are not hearing bursts of forced air either in or out). While you are continuing to breathe, walk through your various body parts mentally willing them to relax. In just a couple of minutes, this simple exercise should have an immediate impact on the level of tension in your body while freeing your mind and improving your overall performance. You can do this even while remaining actively engaged in whatever else you are doing,

Assess yourself in tension management. Circle how you feel you are doing. On this subject, I:

Need a lot of work	Need a little work	Am okay	Feel good where I am

How is tension negatively affecting your performance? What are you going to do to minimize tension in those situations?

_____

_____

_____

Managing the Gap between Strengths and Weaknesses Increases Your Odds of Success

There are many self-development books and advisors that proclaim that you should focus on your strengths; develop your strengths and don't worry about your weaknesses. This is a great story to tell because it is one everyone wants to hear. Who wants to be told that they should work on what they feel inadequate about in themselves or their abilities? In other words, it is easy to get people pumped up about spending time concentrating on what they do well and discard what they do poorly and leave it for someone else.

I am not suggesting that you need to be good at everything and I absolutely believe you should develop your strengths. But my experience is that people naturally do that—everyone wants to show off and challenge their exceptional skills and attributes. Strengths get used, and therefore developed, because they are the most satisfying to engage. So, your strengths will naturally get stronger. However, I believe that if you don't constantly develop your weaknesses, the small gap between your strengths and weaknesses will slowly grow into a giant chasm that will ultimately become your personal albatross.

Let me share a couple of stories. It is common for me to see both new and experienced students emphasizing their best martial arts techniques during warm-ups and class. Why? The answer is simple: you get immediate positive reinforcement when you do something well (for instance, instructors making positive comments or your seeing that you are better at something than others around you), and negative reinforcement when you do something poorly (like being embarrassed as you fall on the floor attempting a technique or someone coming up to correct you). Consider this scenario. John will give us an exercise to do in class, which could be as straightforward as repeating a specific kick over and over. Everyone almost instantly gravitates to using his or her good leg for kicking (yes, in martial arts as in life, we all seem to be blessed with one limb that is seemingly more responsive to our mental instructions than the other). Then, after minutes of positive experiences with the good leg, students will switch and start kicking with the other leg (the bad leg). For obvious reasons, this effort is not nearly as gratifying and it doesn't take long before students will switch back to the good leg to work on it some more. It is funny, when John walks back into the training area, almost everyone switches back to kicking with their good leg to optimize the possibility for public praise and minimize the need for correction. The result: the good leg gets stronger at a much faster pace than the bad leg, which creates a larger and larger gap in kicking ability between them.

The problem is that while your strengths may give you the best chance for success, your weaknesses just as quickly will provide openings for failure. Or, put another way, while your strength may be powerful, your weaknesses will make you vulnerable. In martial arts, your strengths often allow you some quick short-term victories, but with a good opponent, it is your weaknesses that will ultimately determine your fate. Playing basketball, I was a guard—a short one—and could dribble confidently only to my left. Guess what? As soon as my opponents realized this, the defenders would overplay me so that I had to go to my right, which quickly minimized the impact I could make in the game.

I am not suggesting that your weaknesses need to be improved so that they are equal to your strengths. What I am saying is that if your weaknesses are too weak, your strengths won't be able to compensate for them. In basketball, I didn't need to be a great dribbler with my right hand. I simply needed to be good enough that when I was vastly overplayed, my opponent's defensive maneuver would become an opportunity for me.

As well, strengths become weaknesses when overly relied upon. One of my clients is the best negotiator I know. He is so good at it that he negotiates everything, from the deals he cuts with his suppliers, the agreements he makes with his customers, and the arrangements he has with his employees. However, he overuses his strength—as do many when they are uniquely talented at something. Watching him operate on one hand is a thing of beauty. On the other hand, he couldn't create more chaos if he lit himself on fire every morning. One-off deals are constantly made, with individualized timetables, expectations and rewards. So, while his strength is putting together teams and offerings that are exceptional, his weakness is that it is almost impossible for him to align his extraordinary resources to support the changing goals of his company. Everyone is operating to maximize the particulars of his or her own one-off deal which requires the organization to relentlessly work around and overcome, which turns out to be more costly and far less efficient.

When you consider that the risk you are trying to manage is the size of the gap between your strengths and weaknesses, it becomes easier to put in the effort to ensure that you are not overly exposed. Leverage your strengths, but vigilantly develop your weaknesses so that you can at least maintain the skill gap between them. The most direct way I can say this is

Your strengths will help you win, but it is your weaknesses that will ensure you don't.

Assess yourself on whether you regularly strengthen your weaknesses. Circle how you feel you are doing. On this subject, I:

Need a lot of work	Need a little work	Am okay	Feel good where I am

What weaknesses have I been overlooking that need to attention and improvement? What gaps between my strengths and weaknesses position me to fail?

_____

_____

_____

A Strength Can Also Become a Weakness

While there are many lessons in martial arts that repeat themselves, the idea that a strength can also become a weakness is a commonly recurring one. But it doesn't make sense—how could a strength ever be bad? Well, here are a couple of examples.

I enjoy my life, but I like to work! As an overachiever, I work all of the time and many days I am consumed with tasks I want to accomplish. Even when I play, I approach play like work—I want to be a better martial artist, better golfer, better skier. Do you remember my hike up El Yunque? Are you starting to see the weakness here? I can be so driven that without an objective or a goal, I can quickly lose interest. For example, I drive a hybrid. Only those who drive hybrid vehicles will identify with what I am going to say, but once an overachiever has a second by second feedback mechanism that updates you on your miles per gallon usage, it almost becomes a competition to see how many miles you can squeeze out of a gallon of gas. I got to the point that every time I would drive my car, I would create significant useless and unproductive stress trying to at least maintain or beat my highest miles per gallon performance. I know it will come as no surprise that my drive to improve has been and still is one of my strengths. But it was not as obvious to me until I started writing this book how that same drive was creating unnecessary frustration in my life as well.

As we discussed earlier, being entrepreneurial is a strength, but with success, it can quickly become a weakness. My client's superior negotiation skills are a strength, but applied all of the time, these skills have become his weakness. Another common example I find is someone who is a great motivator, but a terrible manager. Though motivators are fantastic at getting everyone excited and wanting to do their best, it is not uncommon for these same leaders to avoid conflict and create limited accountability because they don't like having these more negative conversations. While any strength will offer advantages in specific situations, a strength applied to almost every situation will equally and sometimes more devastatingly become a weakness. The message here is two-fold. First, be aware that your strengths will also surface in specific situations as your weaknesses. And second, the more you over-rely and over-apply your strengths, the greater chance those strengths have of becoming a weakness and undermining your overall progress towards your goals (therefore, negatively impinging on your feelings of success or happiness).

Assess yourself on whether you over-rely on your strengths turning them into weaknesses. Circle how you feel you are doing. On this subject, I:

Need a lot of work	Need a little work	Am okay	Feel good where I am

What strengths do I have that I am not recognizing as weaknesses as they create unnecessary chaos in my life? What strengths am I applying to almost every situation that is having diminishing returns in their effectiveness?

_____

_____

_____

Harmonize—Don't Just Clash and Resist

A college professor I know has had a difficult time harmonizing as his approach always escalated to clashing and resisting. And no, this isn't a story about Michaelle in disguise, but someone else I had the pleasure of getting to know. He had a definite approach to teaching and was good at it. He believed in setting very high standards for his students and passing only those who achieved a specific level of excellence. In almost any school, this value system would be praised. The problem didn't arise from his philosophy, but from that professor's rigidity as to how to apply it. For example, to him, this high standard was best demonstrated through the completion of vast amounts of homework, no grading curve based on class results, and strict class policies. These tactics alienated a large portion of his students. The school, while supportive of maintaining high standards, also had a value system that believed the customer (the student) should be nurtured and satisfied with his or her education. So, it is easy to see the clash forming as the university would compare the professor's performance against the students' evaluations of him.

The university confronted the professor and asked for a compromise in his teaching tactics. The professor, rigid in his thinking, responded something to the effect of, "The way I teach my classes is fine. If you would recruit better students, they wouldn't have such a difficult time making good grades." As you can imagine, that attitude did not go over well. But, the real problem was that no one was happy with this situation. Not only was the university upset with the professor, but the professor was miserable because he was constantly choosing a path of clashing and resisting rather than harmonizing and responding. The professor lost sight of his job, which was to work for the university to achieve their goals. He also lost sight of an even more important fundamental, which is that there are an abundance of quality approaches to teaching that would still deliver the high standards he set and would also provide the more positive and nurturing environment that the students and university desired. The professor got caught up in his way being the "right way," and because he couldn't let go of that, any other way had to be the "wrong way."

This reminds me of numerous coaching sessions I have had with a variety of CFOs over the years. Business requirements, and the work to comply with those standards, have steadily increased over the past few decades. As well, the need to reduce overhead costs in order for companies to run leaner has progressively amplified during this same period. It is no wonder the CFOs, who are typically in charge of accounting, technology, and sometimes operations, are under pressure to do more every day with less. The problem that arises stems from clashing and resisting instead of harmonizing and responding. For example, instead of trying to understand the needs of the executive management group and trying to find alternatives that would work, when approached with additional requirements, the CFOs would often simply respond with, "We can't do that," or "That is impossible to do." The fact is ... if the management team was unwilling to bend on their requirements, *and* unwilling to change the resources being allocated, *and* unwilling to change the existing outputs expected, then the CFOs were likely correct in their statements given that they were probably operating lean to begin with. But I have been around those situations for a long, long time and only in very rare circumstances were the management teams this unreasonable. In the very few circumstances when I found an unreasonable management team, my advice to the CFO was *run*! But back to our topic, here is the advice I have given hundreds of times:

Don't be a box! Become a funnel!

I then followed that statement with something like this:

Anytime your boss asks you to add something significant to your list of duties, don't just thoughtlessly pile it into your box as if you are being asked to make another sacrifice to keep your job. Take time to

- understand the new request,
- create a list of the outputs you currently produce or activities that require substantial time,
- consider the time required for each of those projects or processes,
- prioritize them,
- match them against the resources you have,

- determine what resource changes you would need in order to complete all the work assigned, and
- identify projects and processes that you could either hand off to other people or groups or stop doing altogether.

In the case of the CFOs, once the analysis is done, they are in a position to sit down with the management team (which they are normally part of in the first place) and review the various alternatives that would facilitate the completion of the newly assigned tasks. Once the review is done as outlined above, the solution typically comes down to either a choice of growing the box (the company providing more resources to the CFO in the form of money, people, technology, and so forth), or allowing some less important work to fall out of the bottom of the box (doing away with the work or shifting it to another department). I regularly tell my clients that they need to shift their mindsets from being a box to becoming a funnel (instead of letting everything pile up and loading them down, look for the least important stuff and let it slide out the bottom). Both alternatives—receiving additional resources or cutting out other less valuable work—are good for the CFO. The only alternative that is bad for the career of the CFO is the instinctive reply of "No, we can't do that!" And what drives that philosophical approach is the rigidity that overachievers have to defaulting to being a fixed-sized box.

Thinking you are a box that doesn't have room for one more idea or objective is about resistance and clashing. Thinking you are a funnel and always considering other ideas or objectives and then if the priority is high enough, determining what should be let go of or fall through the bottom is an example of harmonizing. The rigidity of the professor's thinking that his way was the only good way to meet the high standard requirement he desired was about clashing and putting up barriers between him and the school. Taking a harmonizing approach to solve this problem would start with looking for common ground between the professor's objective of maintaining high standards while simultaneously meeting the university's requirement of developing a satisfied and nurtured student body. Unfortunately, in the case of the professor, this was not the end that occurred. The professor maintained his rigidity and lost sight of the fact that he was working for the university, not the other way around. As would be expected, that professor has moved on, not because the university wanted to run him off, but rather because the professor wanted to clash his way to his desired outcome.

Harmonizing instead of clashing can help you work better and find success or happiness more quickly. As you move from thinking you are a fixed-sized box to either a funnel or an expandable box, you will see requests and change as opportunity rather than oppression. When you adopt harmonization as your baseline approach, you will find that you create far less chaos and you are much better able to leverage the existing momentum around you to your advantage.

Assess yourself on whether you default to Harmonizing, or instead Clashing and Resisting. Circle how you feel you are doing. On this subject, I:

Need a lot of work	Need a little work	Am okay	Feel good where I am

In what areas of my life have I become a box and need to learn to become a funnel? In what aspects of my life am I interacting with rigidity rather than with harmony in mind?

_____

_____

_____

What Is the Best Use of Your Time Right Now?

All of us, no matter what our income, gender, race, religion, origin, have the same amount of time—24 hours in a day, 365 days in a year. Each of us has the same capacity. The question is how we use it. For most of us, you can carve out roughly 3,000 of those hours for sleep. Even if you don't need eight hours, you need some time to sleep, and that number cuts a big hole into your available capacity.

From there, you have to decide what to do with the rest of your availability. Choices have consequences, so be aware of the impact your decisions will make. For example, if you need to crunch out a lot of work in the next 120 hours, then you will likely be robbing time from your sleep, your family, physical activity to stay in shape, and other normal daily activities. While this is likely not a problem in the short-term, the longer you stretch your capacity in an unbalanced way, the more you are putting at risk. For instance, if you ignore your family for four months because you allowed work to consume you, don't be surprised if your family drifts away from you. At some point of neglect, they could drift far enough away that permanent damage will occur in those relationships. Or, if you don't take regular care of your body and stay in shape, don't be surprised when you have low energy, weight gain, health problems, and more. Experiencing overloads in one aspect of life over another is normal for overachievers; the key is to not let them get too out of balance for too long.

I remember reading the old book *How to Get Control of Your Time and Your Life* by Alan Lakein. It was part of our reading assignment when I joined IBM in my 20's. And though I have forgotten most everything I read, I will always remember the question that Alan posed to help manage one's life and time, which was this:

What is the best use of my time right now?

The question wasn't about what "to-do's" I could easily cross off of my list, or how many line items I could complete in the shortest amount of time, but rather, what is the best use of my time *right now*. This is about operating in the present. It is about making headway on whatever is important to you rather than always allowing the urgent to consume all available resources. Since we all have the same capacity, doesn't it make sense that the focus should be on using your time effectively every day regardless of what you are doing (relaxation, work, relationships, staying in shape, and so on)? When you take this approach, you will find yourself maximizing your capacity and living a happier, healthier, sustainable life style. But through it all, also be accepting of the notion that we make trade-offs every day as we manage the many objectives that are important to us. When you find frustration in where you are, which can occur often, just answer the question regarding the best use of your time right now; this will help get you back on your path, putting one foot in front of the other until you get there.

Assess yourself on how regularly you ask yourself what is the best use of my time right now. Circle how you feel you are doing. On this subject, I:

Need a lot of work	Need a little work	Am okay	Feel good where I am

How often do I find myself spending a lot of time on issues that are not that important to me but I just want to cross them off my list? What am I avoiding that is the best use of my time, but it seems overwhelming to approach?

_____

_____

_____

Focus on Changing You—Not Everyone Else

"Focus on Changing You" is another important technique to embrace. For your life to change in a meaningful way, it is about you changing—not anyone else. While this sounds cliché, it is absolutely true. As a consultant, I work with organizations helping them with everything from improving operating processes to succession. Because every project I am involved in requires me to deal with a number of different personalities, if I want the client to achieve a successful outcome, it becomes critical for our team members to understand the following premise:

Change occurs when you *change!*

As you know from my previous discussions, I believe change occurs as soon as you start thinking differently. What often gets in our way are feelings of inequity. For example, I will hear comments like, "Why should I change when I already do more than everyone else?" or "I will be happy to change once I see others starting to commit the same level of effort I am already delivering." The problem is that this thinking is flawed. Part of the disconnect with expecting others to "work at your level" before *you* change is that the odds are high that your perceptions are wrong, both of yourself and of others. The gap between your effort or contribution and that of others is rarely as wide as you imagine. Quite frankly, it may be the reverse because you might actually be taking far more than you are giving. How could this be? The reason is very logical:

We give ourselves credit for everything we think, say, and do.

We only give others credit for what we see them do.

This is a really important concept to embrace and one most people resist, so I am going to take you through a simple scenario. Let's say you had a project that had the deadline of last Friday. Because you were not done by 5:30 pm (your normal quitting time on Friday), you decided to stay late (until 9:00 pm) and get it done before you left. After leaving that evening, frustrated by this last minute requirement, you spent your drive time home and some time that evening pondering how this intense scrambling could have been avoided. Over the weekend, you found yourself continuing this mental dialogue and were excited when you came up with a few ideas worth trying to minimize the chances of this situation repeating itself.

On a different track, earlier that same week, you noticed a co-worker who was clearly struggling to meet a different project deadline. After surmising this, you extended an offer to stay and help if necessary. Your co-worker thanked you for your generosity, but declined the need for assistance. So, in this simplistic case study, you are likely to give yourself credit for the following:

- 3.5 hours of Friday evening work to get your project out on time,
- At least 1 hour of think time Friday night trying to come up with ideas as to how to avoid this situation in the future,
- A couple of hours of think time over the weekend to arrive at a couple of ideas worth trying to avoid this situation in the future,
- And bonus time for your willingness to stay and help out your co-worker, even though you did not actually stay.

Let me be clear. You deserve to give yourself credit for all of this effort and willingness. If you are like most of us, with each exceptional effort, you make a quick deposit in your imaginary "I Am Valuable" bank account. The bottom line is that for the week in question, you probably felt like you put in a minimum of six extra hours with a willingness to do even more, with the value-add of some creative efficiency ideas to boot. The problem comes when you compare your effort to that of, let's say, your co-worker who was in a similar situation (whom you offered to help). First, from a common overachiever's lens, you probably assumed that your co-worker only stayed for an extra hour or two maximum. Second, you might have diminished your co-worker's effort even further by thinking about how disorganized he or she was and had that been you with your superior skills, the late night effort would not have even been required. Third, no one else was the kind of team player you were and offered to help you. So, huge chasms are constantly being created in our minds when we compare ourselves to others because of our flawed and invalid perceptions.

How can there ever really be equity in our business or personal life when we always give ourselves credit for everything we think, do, and say and only give credit back for what we actually see others do? If this wasn't bad enough, we are likely to discount the effort we see from others with thoughts such as (1) they didn't put in the same level of caring or effort we did, or (2) they should put in more time given their lesser abilities as it takes them longer to do the same work we do. Even with what we see, our egos often get in the way of a realistic or accurate self-report as we inflate our efforts and diminish the efforts of those around us. As humans, we pay a lot of attention to ourselves, and don't pay that much attention to anyone else, so this contribution gap we hold on to as our excuse for not changing first is mostly fantasy.

There are multiple messages in this section. The most important one is that *you* need to change first! It is also likely that you will have to change second and third as well. The reason is straightforward. If you want anything in your life to be different, the only person you have a chance of controlling is yourself. The second message is ... the odds are high that you have given yourself a higher value for your efforts than you deserve. Even if you haven't, you still need to consider the idea that you might be diminishing the value that others are providing around you.

Assess yourself on whether you focus on changing you first or others. Circle how you feel you are doing. On this subject, I:

Need a lot of work	Need a little work	Am okay	Feel good where I am

In what areas of your life are you likely giving others less value than they deserve? What changes to yourself do you need to consider making now?

_____

_____

_____

Don't Be Someone Else's Rug

In the 70's, there was a big movement in business culture to learn to be more assertive, aptly called "assertiveness training." Michaelle was quick to enroll because this was an important skill set to call upon, especially with many women moving into jobs that had historically been held by men (Michaelle was a systems engineer with IBM during this period). The concept was simple: "You need to speak your mind, ask for what you want, demand what is fair, and don't let yourself be a rug for everyone to step on." In our early years working at IBM together, when one of the secretaries needed to step away or take a break, she would often come over to Michaelle and ask her to cover with typing, answering the phone, and so on. In addition to the fact that she held the professional job of being a systems specialist, Michaelle also had earned her undergraduate degree in psychology and an MBA with a concentration in accounting. I just had a bachelor's degree in business—far less educated—yet no one ever asked me to fill in.

About 95% of the time, whoever they asked to fill in usually did it (always women, most often in paraprofessional roles), complaining and upset with themselves for agreeing to do it. Yet, Michaelle rarely agreed to fill in. She was nice about it, but assertive about the fact that she had other matters and duties to attend to. This was not an issue that some people were nice and some weren't—it was a matter that most of us, when specifically asked to do something, regardless of how unfair the request is, tend to do it. Assertiveness training, to me, helped many people understand that disagreeing or saying "no" was not about creating conflict, merely setting appropriate boundaries, especially when someone else was inappropriately crossing those boundaries. When I asked Michaelle why she so often declined, her comment in confidence (which I am kind-of betraying now with her reluctant consent) was that she had worked hard to earn her MBA and her current professional position in IBM. She commented that men were inclined at that time to want to pigeon hole women into administrative roles and therefore she had to walk a tighter line than a man would, distancing herself from that perception in order to maintain her professional status. Trust me when I tell you she was right. While Michaelle was privileged to have entered the professional workforce at a time when many before her had been required to fight some very difficult crusades, many today take for granted the constant battles women like Michaelle had to face to earn today's closer-to-balanced respect you find in the workplace.

Today, you don't hear much about assertiveness training. When this was popular, it was a different time. When people, especially women, were regularly being inappropriately pushed around by those willing to be confrontational and aggressive, being assertive first became critical for survival, and later a foundational skill for success.

I want to point out, however, the distinct difference between being assertive and being a bully (or overly aggressive). In my view, being assertive is about speaking up for yourself, asking for reasonable accommodation and many other examples of one person asking for fair treatment from another. However, many people overlook the aspect of fairness of this powerful technique and simply become aggressive about demanding whatever they want, even when they know they will be taking unfair advantage of someone, or some company, when they get what they are asking for. The bottom line is that most people will acquiesce to those making demands simply to avoid uncomfortable confrontation. While it is important for you to learn to be assertive and to demand to be treated fairly or with respect, in my opinion, it is equally important for you to not use this powerful technique to take advantage of others just because you can.

For those who are wondering how to resolve the seeming contradiction between being assertive and harmonizing, I have included two examples to clarify why these two concepts are not in conflict with each other. Understand that assertiveness and conflict are no more synonymous than are harmonizing and surrender (giving up or rolling-over). You can easily be assertive while harmonizing.

One example would be the often discussed notion that a common strategy in martial arts is to take advantage of the force of your opponent. This idea is about harmonizing and allowing your attackers to do what they want—then taking advantage of whatever they do. This technique is not about rolling over or giving up, but rather waiting for openings or weaknesses to present themselves so that you can end the engagement.

Another example of how assertiveness and harmonizing work together is in the negotiation process. There are hundreds of books out on this topic, but one of the books I like is *Getting to Yes* by Roger Fisher and William Ury. They walk you through the idea that soft bargaining (trying to be friends, yielding to pressure, accepting one-sided losses to reach agreement) is just as bad as hard bargaining (participants are adversaries, the goal is victory, distrust others and apply pressure). They recommend negotiating using "principled negotiation." In principled negotiation, the parties negotiating are to take on the role of problem-solvers, not people just trying to win. The focus is on exploring what each side is looking to achieve rather than the positions currently being taken. The goal is to find a win-win solution by inventing options for mutual gain (expanding the universe of benefits). The point is...the authors suggest being assertive regarding the desire to find solutions to address the problems (they call this being "hard on the problem"), but harmonize with each other to find win-win scenarios (they call this being "soft on the people"). Far too often, I see people being assertive and clashing (rather than harmonizing) or timid and harmonizing as these two combinations often create lose-win or lose-lose alternatives. Based on my experience, in most cases, there is a win-win alternative sitting there waiting to be found if you take the time to look for it by using principled negotiation which is soft on the people (harmonizing) and hard on the problem (assertive).

Assess yourself on being someone else's rug. Circle how you feel you are doing. On this subject, I:

| Need a lot of work | Need a little work | Am okay | Feel good where I am |

What areas of my life do I need to do a better job standing up for myself? How can I learn to incorporate both harmonization and assertiveness together more often?

_____

_____

_____

Aligning What We Think With What We Do

Look for disconnects between what you think and do. And when you find yourself taking an action that contradicts the way you have been thinking, take a moment to figure out why there is a disconnect. When your actions and thoughts are not in congruence, know that you are setting yourself up to get stuck. Doesn't it make sense that a major source of dissatisfaction can occur anytime you are thinking one way yet acting another? If we can't be honest with ourselves ... how can we ever expect to know who we really are and what is really important to us? This is simply about building consistency and trust into the way each of us make decisions and live our lives.

For example, it is pretty common for overachievers to tell me that they want to stop working so hard and allocate some time to get into better shape. But many continue working all hours of the day and evening, and then go home, go to bed, and do it all over again. Clearly there is a conflict between what is being said to me and what the clients are actually doing. Now it could be that the clients wish to be in better shape but don't want to do the work, so there really isn't a disconnect. But for some, they are truly torn. Some overachievers are almost obsessive-compulsive about their work and they don't know how to turn that part of themselves off. It is as if they almost have to become obsessive about something else in order to make the transition. So, if this sounds like you, whatever it is that you want to do that you are not doing, don't try to eat the entire elephant in one bite. Take a baby step. If you want to get in better shape and you are struggling to make the change, start by doing sit-ups or something for five minutes in the morning—just five minutes. Maybe add something else, like a few pushups several weeks later. Build on incremental success. But don't try to make up for lost time or achieve a month's worth of strengthening in three days. If you do, all that is likely to happen is that you are going to hurt yourself and quickly be back to doing nothing again.

If you still are having trouble making the change you want, find yourself a support group either close to home or between work and home (for convenience) to help you stay on track. For me, the martial arts school fills this role because classes start at a specific time so I have to plan around them. As well, I have friends at the school I look forward to seeing and training with. When I am scheduled to teach, I need to show up because I have a job to do. As a workaholic, without this type of regimen, I would work each day fully intending to work out each evening, with each evening ending the same way—an unhealthier Bill. The point is ... when you find inconsistencies, address them as they arise, and either replan or reprioritize how you are spending your time. The more quickly you can align what you are thinking with what you are doing, the more efficient your work, the more effective your effort, and the more rapid the accomplishment of your desired results. And just as important, resolving inconsistencies is a great way to avoid feeling unhappy or unsuccessful about whatever it is you are trying to achieve.

Assess yourself on aligning what you think with what you do. Circle how you feel you are doing. On this subject, I:

Need a lot of work	Need a little work	Am okay	Feel good where I am

What actions am I taking today that are inconsistent with what I think? What do I think that I never do? What steps can I take to align these inconsistencies and start making progress towards what is important to me?

_____

_____

_____

"What You *Are* Doing" Wrap-Up

The focus of this chapter has been techniques that can help you reconsider whether what you are doing is the best approach for accomplishing what you are wanting. Hopefully, at least one of the techniques in this chapter will help you identify what you want to let go of so that you can make the changes necessary to get you unstuck. Because this path was in response to a negative evaluation earlier as to your progress or priorities, it is time to reassess whether the best action to get you back on track to what is important to you would be to **replan, reprioritize,** or **reaffirm** your Desire. The following flowchart will provide insight as to where you are in the Process and where each choice will take you, to help you regain your lost momentum.

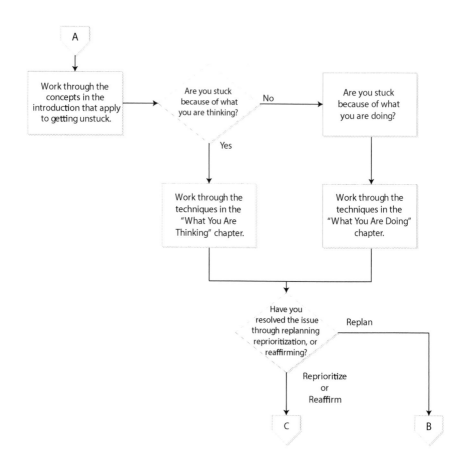

Chapter 7
Conclusion

Everything included in this text is designed to help you become more aware of yourself, more aware of how you both propel and sabotage your own desires and efforts, and how to better harness the power of momentum into progress. This book is meant to facilitate the building of your self-evaluation and reaction skills to the point that when you determine you are feeling unsuccessful or unhappy about your progress or priorities, you can call upon the Process and its Techniques at a high level allowing you to alter your desires, plans, tactics, priorities, the way you work and the way you are thinking to quickly resolve your dissatisfaction and find the success and happiness you are attempting to achieve. But as you work through this Process, keep this in mind:

> *Regarding some objectives, you will begin to see a pattern of the same issue coming up over and over again in different settings creating dissatisfaction. While a technique might dissolve the frustration in the short-term, when you find yourself getting stuck on the same issue repetitively, it is most likely because you have been unwilling to let go of something you think you know.*

Taking a High-Level Jog Through the Process

As you know by now, I believe that the core of whatever dissatisfaction you are struggling with is centered in Desire. Once you have identified what you want and have created a plan with tactics, realistic timeframes, and reasonable expectations, it's time to go to work. You imagine it, take the incremental steps, put in the effort and then you achieve your objective. Much of the time, this is all there is to it. But because many overachiever objectives are complex or ambitious, the Process focuses in on the evaluation step because we are notorious for constantly assessing our progress.

As long as we are happy or feeling successful about our progress or priorities, we are good about keeping our heads down and continuing to do good work. However, problems arise anytime we start feeling dissatisfied with where we are. Therefore, it is important to watch for and be ready to respond to the early warning signals as they occur, like loss of momentum, diminishing returns, or functional disconnect. By quickly reacting to these signals, you can avoid the negative path of getting stuck by figuring out what to let go of and utilizing the action steps of replanning, reprioritizing, and reaffirming to maintain constant momentum towards your goal. And if you want to even further protect yourself from getting stuck, set up routine self-diagnostics at certain designated intervals within an objective to take a close look at how your plan, work, and progress are syncing up. Doing this preventive maintenance procedure of replanning, reprioritizing, or reaffirming before any early warning signals are fired allows you to less emotionally make the necessary alterations to stave off dissatisfaction and sustain your momentum.

Once the early warning signals start firing, they will get louder and brighter until they eventually create enough pain (dissatisfaction and frustration regarding your perceived success or happiness) for you to respond to them. At this point, you have two paths to follow to get you back on course. It is time to consider "What You *Are* Thinking" (chapter 5) and "What You *Are* Doing" (chapter 6). By embracing a technique or two from these chapters, which are designed to help you determine what to let go of that you think you know, you will find yourself either consciously or subconsciously replanning, reprioritizing, or reaffirming in order to regain your momentum.

If your solution is to replan, then you join back into the flow at the Desire step (chapter 2) to re-think or fine-tune what you want as well as your plan to get there. If reprioritizing or reaffirming is the answer, your updated perspective allows you to jump right back into the Try (Work)-Evaluation loop making progress again.

But as I stated in chapter 2, "Desire," it is critical to understand that when you pinpoint something you want to achieve, unless getting stuck *is* your objective, you need to embrace the idea that as you move towards your goal, you can expect and should be open to replanning, reprioritizing, or reaffirming your desire as part of your normal process to achieve. The moment your plan is static and unchangeable, the second you take on a rigid approach to doing the work, the instant you lock in your current priorities, you will have started down a path to getting stuck.

Experiential Exercise

Based on the fact that you decided to read this book, and since you have reached this point, I thought it might be helpful to incorporate a summary exercise for you to work through. By thinking through the sections of the exercise, you will get a detailed look at how the Process works and how you can work the Process. This exercise is not meant to frustrate or deter you from any goal you want to achieve. And if you start feeling that way as you work through it, you might be experiencing an early warning signal to getting stuck. If this is the case, just go back and reread the last two chapters ("What You *Are* Thinking" and "What You *Are* Doing") to see if that triggers an idea that you should let go of. This should help you return to the exercise to continue working through it.

My exercise starts off by asking you to identify the top five goals you want to accomplish (desires) over the next three years. Since the most common frustration points I experience working with overachievers is either an unrealistic timeframe or unreasonable expectations, I devised this exercise to provide you with some additional perspective. By the way, I regularly use a variation of this format in strategic planning with my clients not only to ensure that their strategies, resources, and expectations are in alignment, but to verify that their available resources are ample enough to achieve their strategies and expectations. When a disconnect is identified between these three, the action to resolve is always the same: replan, reprioritize, or reaffirm.

What are the Desires (up to five plans or objectives) you want to accomplish in the next three years?

1. _____

_____

_____

_____

_____

_____

(continued)

2. _____
_____
_____
_____
_____
_____
_____

3. _____
_____
_____
_____
_____
_____
_____

4. _____
_____
_____
_____
_____
_____

5. _____
_____
_____
_____
_____
_____

For each Desire identified, jot down some high level plans and plan tactics. As well, for each plan tactic, consider the timeframe (how many hours you believe each tactic will require). By the way, consider doubling whatever hours come to mind because it is not uncommon for us (overachievers) to be far too optimistic in this area.

Objective 1

Anticipated
Hours

    Plan Tactics: _____   _____

                _____   _____

                _____   _____

                _____   _____

                _____   _____

    Plan Expectations: _____

                      _____

                      _____

                      _____

                      _____

                      _____

                      _____

Objective 2

Anticipated
Hours

    Plan Tactics: _____   _____

                _____   _____

                _____   _____

                _____   _____

                _____   _____

    Plan Expectations: _____

                      _____

                      _____

                      _____

                      _____

                      _____

                      _____

(continued)

Objective 3

Anticipated
Hours

Plan Tactics: _____ _____

_____ _____

_____ _____

_____ _____

_____ _____

Plan Expectations: _____

_____

_____

_____

_____

_____

_____

Objective 4

Anticipated
Hours

Plan Tactics: _____ _____

_____ _____

_____ _____

_____ _____

Plan Expectations: _____

_____

_____

_____

_____

_____

_____

Objective 5   Anticipated
                                                                           Hours

    Plan Tactics: _____ _____

                      _____ _____

                      _____ _____

                      _____ _____

                      _____ _____

    Plan Expectations: _____

                            _____

                            _____

                            _____

                            _____

                            _____

                            _____

Now it is time to summarize the hours for each plan as well as to identify a rough date of completion. Fill in the blanks below to give yourself an idea about your current thinking.

Objective 1:   Expected Hours   Expected
                to Complete: _____ Completion Date: _____

Objective 2:   Expected Hours   Expected
                to Complete: _____ Completion Date: _____

Objective 3:   Expected Hours   Expected
                to Complete: _____ Completion Date: _____

Objective 4:   Expected Hours   Expected
                to Complete: _____ Completion Date: _____

Objective 5:   Expected Hours   Expected
                to Complete: _____ Completion Date: _____

Next, let's consider your available capacity. Overachievers are often overly optimistic about our available capacity. So, I put together a very simple form to get you to think about how much time you have already committed, which will then give you a better idea about the amount of time available to you to accomplish new objectives. This set of exercises is intended to help you consider personal capacity outside of work, but you can refocus the exercises to identify your work desires, timeframes, and expectations and then compare that information against your total uncommitted work hours. So let's get started.

Total Hours Available (365 days, 24 hours per day):   8,760

Total Hours Expected for Sleeping (2,920 is 8 hours per day)   _____

Total Hours Sick (5 days, 16 hours a day (because sleep was already counted above), is 80 hours)   _____

Total Vacation Days (14 days, 16 hours a day, is 224)   _____

Total Work Hours assuming 5 days a week 49 weeks a year, 40 hours per week (removing 2 weeks' vacation and 1 week sick time, is 1,960)   _____

Morning grooming to get ready (1 hour 365 days a year is 365)   _____

Eating (3 meals a day, 30 minutes each, 365 days a year is 548 rounded up a half an hour)   _____

Commute time between home and work and back (1 hour 245 days a year which removes sick days, vacations and weekends, is 245)   _____

Quality time with your family (1 hour a day 365 days a year, is 365)   _____

Time to work out and stay in shape (30 minutes a day 4 days a week plus commute or warm up/cool down time totaling one hour a day 49 weeks a year, is, 196)   _____

Household chores, including bill paying, repairs, maintenance, etc. (3 hours a week, 49 weeks a year, is 147)   _____

Time to relax, watch TV, come down from the day, get ready for bed (1.5 hours a day, 365 days a year, is 548 rounded up a half an hour)   _____

Time Available for You to Achieve Your Goals   _____

If you used all of the defaults (which would result to about 1,162 hours available), you ended up with a very conservative number because most overachievers work more than 8 hours a day, 5 days a week. We often don't take a lot of sick time (but then my default was only 5 days total), and many overachievers struggle to take 2 full weeks of vacation (although they may be entitled to 3, 4, or 5 weeks off). As well, this version of the form doesn't factor in time to take care of kids, spend with your spouse, and spend on other important activities like religion, volunteer work, and so on. This example was meant to get you started thinking about your capacity, but you can create a customized version that works for you.

I also recognize that you can create more capacity by doubling or tripling up the number of objectives met with a single activity. For example, if you exercise with your family, you are spending quality time with your family while taking care of your health needs. If you eat dinner with a client, you are taking care of both work and nourishment activities at the same time. If part of your vacation is spent with both family and clients, you could triple up by building work relationships, spending quality time with family, and enjoying down time or recreational activities together. As you can see, with a little creativity, you can come up with a number of ways to leverage currently committed time (or create additional capacity).

For me, as well as a lot of overachievers, we pick up some extra time by not always getting enough sleep. Different people have different needs when it comes to the right amount of sleep required to wake up refreshed and ready for the day. But whatever that sleep requirement is, as you move from ample sleep to sleep deprivation, you have a very high chance of experiencing consequences in the form of marginal productivity, excessive mistakes, muddled thinking, and other negative outcomes.

When I go through this exercise, after considering my normal work schedule, sleep, working out, five sick days, a typical golf and skiing schedule, morning and evening routines, required ongoing household chores and nourishment, I have only about 850 hours left available to spend with my family, to spend on vacation, or to spend in other ways. My 850 hours also assumes wonderful efficiency in everything I am doing with no unplanned events, health issues, family problems, or any other chaos consuming my time. As you can imagine, my—as well as anyone's—uncommitted time calculated here could easily be reduced by several hundred hours in the normal course of just managing life.

Now that you have outlined your plans, plan tactics, time requirements, and expectations, compare that with your available capacity. If you have plenty of time, then great, you are ready to move on! But if you are like most of us who go through this, you quickly realize you have a disconnect between what you want and what you have time to accomplish. As you are likely experiencing, even in the beginning of this Process as we convert our desires into actionable plans, replanning or reprioritizing quickly come into play to reconcile capacity, timeframe, and expectations. Common options available to you are to (1) stretch the timeframe to coincide with your availability; (2) change the tactics within your plan to better align with your capacity, or (3) change the priority of your objectives and drop those of lesser priority off your list altogether. The point is—you have a wonderful opportunity to keep yourself from getting stuck simply by going through this kind of thinking process to determine a realistic timeframe and reasonable expectations from the beginning.

Once you have reconciled your time needs and therefore some aspect of your expectations with your available capacity, it is time to start following your plan and doing the work.

Doing the Work (Try): Are there some techniques associated with any of the objectives that you want to keep top of mind that will improve your chances of sustaining your work effort and working better? Are there some preset intervals you want to establish to do a preventive maintenance check to look for emerging signs of the early warning signals or consider the actions of replanning, reprioritizing and reaffirming?

_____

_____

_____

_____

_____

_____

_____

_____

_____

_____

_____

At this point, as long as you remain unstuck and continue with forward momentum, you will continue to experience the Try (Work)-Evaluate loop until you achieve your objective. For that reason, you can step away from the form and just "do the work." However, if you begin feeling dissatisfied in some way (feeling unsuccessful or unhappy about your progress or priorities), reach a preset preventative maintenance analysis point, or encounter any of the early warning signals, it's time to determine what to let go of so that you can utilize the actions steps of replanning, reprioritizing or reaffirming to avoid getting stuck.

Evaluation Point (a negative evaluation or at a preset preventative maintenance analysis point): Are you experiencing any of the early warning signals (loss of momentum, diminishing returns, functional disconnect)? If you are dissatisfied, what are you feeling unhappy or unsuccessful about?

Objective 1: _____

_____

_____

Objective 2: _____

_____

_____

Objective 3: _____

_____

_____

Objective 4: _____

_____

_____

Objective 5: _____

_____

_____

Action Step: After considering the various techniques in chapters 5 ("What You *Are* Thinking") and 6 ("What You *Are* Doing"), what bubbled up? Did this material help you let go of what you thought you knew, positioning you to replan, reprioritize, or reaffirm your desire? If replanning, how did this impact your plan, tactic, timeframe, or expectation? If reprioritizing, how did it impact priority? If reaffirming, what are you going to do to disconnect the emotional link between your plan and your performance?

Objective 1 (jot down your thoughts regarding whichever of the following applies):

Anticipated Hours

Change in Plan
Tactics:
_____   _____

_____   _____

Change in Plan
Expectations:
_____

_____

Change in
Priority:
_____

_____

Change in
Emotional Link:
_____

_____

Objective 2 (jot down your thoughts regarding whichever of the following applies):

Anticipated Hours

Change in Plan
Tactics:
_____   _____

_____   _____

Change in Plan
Expectations:
_____

_____

Change in
Priority:
_____

_____

Change in
Emotional Link:
_____

_____

Objective 3 (jot down your thoughts regarding   Anticipated
whichever of the following applies):   Hours

    Change in Plan
    Tactics: _____   _____

                _____   _____

    Change in Plan
    Expectations: _____

                _____

    Change in
    Priority: _____

                _____

    Change in
    Emotional Link: _____

                _____

Objective 4 (jot down your thoughts regarding   Anticipated
whichever of the following applies):   Hours

    Change in Plan
    Tactics: _____   _____

                _____   _____

    Change in Plan
    Expectations: _____

                _____

    Change in
    Priority: _____

                _____

    Change in
    Emotional Link: _____

                _____

(continued)

Objective 5 (jot down your thoughts regarding whichever of the following applies):	Anticipated Hours
Change in Plan Tactics: _____	_____
_____	_____
Change in Plan Expectations: _____	
_____	
Change in Priority: _____	
_____	
Change in Emotional Link: _____	
_____	

The changes in your thinking or doing with regard to your progress or priorities will determine which form in this summary exercise to cycle back to and rework. If you have decided to replan, then you would cycle back to the beginning of this exercise to the first form, or you might skip to the plan tactics or plan expectations. If you have reconciled your source of dissatisfaction by reprioritizing or reaffirming, then sliding back up to the form under "Doing the Work (Try)" will land you where you need to go.

Time Management Tips for Remaining Unstuck

As I have said before, overachievers tend to

- be overly optimistic about how efficiently they can accomplish any particular activity or objective.
- take care of themselves only after everyone else on their list has been satisfied.

Therefore, while overachievers accomplish great things, they often find themselves stuck because they are suffering from a disconnect between their commitments and available resources. Over commitment combined with our internal pressure for excellence creates a need for a pressure relief valve. Unfortunately, that relief valve is often one or more of the following:

- Sleeping less
- Skipping quality time with our family
- Not exercising
- Eating unhealthy fast food
- Cutting back on the down time we need to rejuvenate

It doesn't take a genius to see where these options will eventually lead and it doesn't end well. Therefore, I am suggesting that you think about the following as you consider the many projects you are trying to accomplish:

- Work first on those projects that are of the highest importance to you.
- When you have multiple high-importance projects in the queue, don't just default to doing a little work on each of them daily. Manage your efforts so that you are spending an optimal amount of productive time to achieve the greatest progress on each.
- Start watching closely for diminishing returns on your efforts. Don't waste significant resources for small incremental gain when that effort is sacrificing other equally high priority objectives.
- Put caps on the amount of time you are willing to commit to certain tasks, projects, or expectations. By creating boundaries, you will likely not only accomplish more with your time, but also be more efficient, given that you are working with identified constraints.
- When you have overcommitted, face up to it right away and accept the consequences early. Don't wait until the last minute, creating excessive stress and frustration trying to force everything to work through personal self-sacrifice.
- Keep in mind that time is the only unreplenishable resource, so don't waste it.

You can save yourself a lot of frustration while simultaneously sustaining your momentum through better time, commitment, and constraint management. This will allow you to move multiple important objectives forward, optimize progress with each, create whatever balance you are looking for between them and avoid the all-to-often chosen self-sacrifice as your solution for getting everything done.

Final Thoughts

Here are a few key highlights to keep in mind to help you find the happiness and success you are looking for:

- Distinguish Desire from Wishing. Desire is characterized by a commitment to action.
- You will feel stuck anytime you are unable to resolve your unhappiness, including feelings of being unsuccessful, regarding your progress or priority.
- Be prepared to reapply the replan-reprioritize-reaffirm cycle as often as a feeling of being stuck arises. The early warning signals for being stuck are loss of momentum, diminishing returns, and functional disconnect.
- The only means of becoming unstuck are changing what you think and changing what you do.
- Let go of what you think you know!

Thanks for the time you have spent reading this book. I hope the Process outlined in this text can provide you with even a portion of the help and insight I have gained by writing it!!

About the Author

**Bill Reeb, CPA, CITP, CGMA,
Co-Founder and CEO,
Succession Institute, LLC**

Bill Reeb has been consulting to all sizes of
businesses, from Mom and Pop operations to
Fortune 100 companies, for three decades. In 1986,
he decided to boost his role as a trusted advisor to
his clients and became a CPA. Prior to his life as
a CPA, he had the exciting experience of working in sales for IBM in the late
1970's. As an entrepreneur, Bill has founded seven small businesses,
including two women's clothing stores, one retail computer software store, a
software development firm, a computer consulting firm, a CPA firm, and his
current management consulting firm, Succession Institue, LLC.

As an award-winning public speaker, Bill lectures throughout the U.S. and
Canada to thousands of executives and CPAs each year. In addition, he has
been featured on numerous video-taped and live television programs. As an
award-winning author, Bill is internationally published with hundreds of
articles and columns to his credit. In addition to this book, Bill's other books
include *Securing the Future: Succession Planning Basics, Securing the Future: Taking
Succession to the Next Level,* and the fourth edition of his consulting book called
*Becoming A Trusted Advisor: How to Add Value, Improve Client Loyalty, and Increase
Profits.*

Bill has served in numerous leadership roles in a variety of organizations as a
volunteer and has been especially active within the CPA profession,
including as a past member of the AICPA Board of Directors. Bill is also
nationally recognized with numerous honors such as one of the top 10 most
recommended CPA firm consultants, *Top 100 Most Influential CPAs,* and other
awards.

Bill enjoys a number of hobbies. He is an avid golfer, skier, and occasional
hiker. However, he spends the majority of his free time teaching, as well as
continually learning, six different styles of martial arts.

Bill relied heavily on the guidance of John Blankenship, his friend and
teacher, while writing this book.

John Blankenship

John has been teaching the science and philosophy of transformation through traditional martial arts for over 40 years. During this time, he has taught, coached, and inspired thousands of professionals leading them through personal change. John lives and trains in Austin, Texas.

Printed in the United States
By Bookmasters